UNSUNG LAND, ASPIRING NATION
JOURNEYS IN BOUGAINVILLE

UNSUNG LAND, ASPIRING NATION

JOURNEYS IN BOUGAINVILLE

GORDON PEAKE

Australian
National
University

ANU PRESS

PACIFIC SERIES

For Patrick

Australian
National
University

ANU PRESS

Published by ANU Press
The Australian National University
Canberra ACT 2600, Australia
Email: anupress@anu.edu.au

Available to download for free at press.anu.edu.au

ISBN (print): 9781760465438
ISBN (online): 9781760465445

WorldCat (print): 1346579423
WorldCat (online): 1346581358

DOI: 10.22459/ULAN.2022

Printed by Lightning Source
ingramcontent.com/publishers-page/environmental-responsibility

Cover design and layout by ANU Press. Cover photograph: Bougainville Referendum Commission/Jeremy Miller.

This book is published under the aegis of the Pacific Editorial Board of ANU Press.

Some names in this book have been changed in the interests of privacy.

Contents

See enough and write it down.

— Joan Didion

Abbreviations and other shortened forms

ABC	Australian Broadcasting Corporation
ABG	Autonomous Bougainville Government
ANU	The Australian National University
ATM	automated teller machine
AusAID	Australian Agency for International Development
BRA	Bougainville Revolutionary Army
COVID	COVID-19 (coronavirus disease of 2019)
DFAT	Department of Foreign Affairs and Trade
JSB	Joint Supervisory Body
MoU	memorandum of understanding
NCOBA	National Coordination Office for Bougainville Affairs
Peace Agreement	Bougainville Peace Agreement
PNG	Papua New Guinea
Reasons	Reasons Bar & Grill
RSL	Returned Services League [Australia]
Tchibo	Tchibo Rock
UN	United Nations

Acknowledgements

Writing this book has been the most wicked and twisted of roads. I owe thanks to a lot of people who helped me reach its end. For reading various drafts and providing encouragement I thank Bobby Anderson, Tom Bamforth, Jim Della-Giacoma, Andrew Harris, Sue Ingram, Christine Kearney, Jono Lineen, Stephanie Lusby, Kylie McKenna, Mark Notaras, Kevin Pullen, Michael Rose and Ceridwen Spark. Nadine Davidoff told me the book I should write and Felicity Tepper helped me wrangle the draft into shape to get it to a publisher. Awaneesh Bamola has been incredibly helpful to me. The two anonymous reviewers provided extremely helpful steer. Anthony Regan read a near-final draft and helped save me from myself. Stewart Firth, Siobhan McDonnell and Emily Tinker at ANU Press helped find the book a worthy home and Glenine Hamlyn has done a top-notch job copyediting the text. I thank the Pacific Manuscripts Bureau of The Australian National University, and the University of Oxford's Pitt Rivers Museum, for giving me access to the archives.

John Timlin, my literary agent, has been incredibly supportive, despite his scepticism about the level of windfalls likely to come from ANU Press's open-access publishing model. Ken Imako from DarkAsidE came up with the book's main title. Any mistakes in the book are my own, as are all the interpretations. The latter do not reflect the views of anyone I worked for.

I wrote the book as a visitor at the School of Regulation and Global Governance at The Australian National University. I loved my time there, and I thank Veronica Taylor and Miranda Forsyth for sponsoring my visitorship.

Daniel Flitton from the *Interpreter*, the blog of the Lowy Institute, gave me the space to test ideas. Earlier versions of some of the material in the book have already been published.[1]

I have a wonderful family support team: Suzanne, and our sons, Charles and Patrick. Suzanne invariably has much more faith in me than I have in myself, and I love her more each day. I don't know how she puts up with me sometimes, but I'm so glad she does.

Our two sons are our proudest achievements. 'Never give up, Dad,' said Charles to me one night when I was unburdening myself to Suzanne about how I feared I would never finish this project. I thought Charles and his brother had gone to bed. As it turned out, he was tuning into our conversation, and his words – delivered with all his passion, all his sincerity – stopped me from abandoning the project. Patrick would ask, 'When's this book you are going to write for me going to be finished, Dad?' I'm happy not to have to fob him off with any more variations on 'Soon', and that instead I can say, 'Now'.

Palisades, Washington D.C.
May 2022

---

1   Gordon Peake, 'The Black Spot', *Island* 149, no. 2 (2017): 52–65; Gordon Peake, 'Bougainville's Autonomy Arrangements: Implementation Dilemmas', *The Round Table: The Commonwealth Journal of International Affairs* 108, no. 3 (2019): 275–92, doi.org/10.1080/00358533.2019.1618610; Gordon Peake and Miranda Forsyth, 'Street-Level Bureaucrats in a Relational State: The Case of Bougainville', *Public Administration and Development* 1, no. 42 (2021): 12–21, doi.org/10.1002/pad.1911. See also Gordon Peake and Ceridwen Spark, 'Australian Aid in Papua New Guinea: Men's Views on Pay Disparities, Power Imbalances and Written Products in the Development Sector', *The Australian Journal of Anthropology* 32, no.1 (2021): 3–18, doi.org/10.1111/taja.12387.

Foreword

Negotiating just and inclusive peace agreements after violent intrastate territorial conflicts, in which there are often multiple parties and myriads of impacts, typically involves long and difficult processes. However, as the title of an edited volume published in 2007 asserts, it is the implementation of such agreements that is 'the real challenge to intrastate peace'.[1] Indeed, on the cover of the book we read the claim that: '[m]ost intrastate peace agreements are implemented inadequately or not at all. This leads to renewed tensions and often to resumption of armed conflict.' The factors involved in the poor record of peace agreement implementation include:

- limited capacity for implementation in both national and subnational political and administrative structures
- resistance by state authorities
- the pressures and demands involved in the need to build entirely new, or fundamentally reformed, post-conflict, subnational government institutions.

Failure in peace agreement implementation is, undoubtedly, one of the reasons why the most recent global analysis of the recurrence of intrastate conflicts showed that around 60 per cent of such conflicts since the Second World War have resumed within five years of the signing of a peace agreement.[2]

---

1   Miek Boltjes, ed., *Implementing Negotiated Agreements: The Real Challenge to Intrastate Peace* (The Hague: T.M.C. Asser Press, 2007).
2   United Nations Office for the Coordination of Human Affairs (OCHA), *Human Security Report 2012: Sexual Violence, Education and War: Beyond the Mainstream Narrative* (Vancouver: Human Security Press, 2012), 171, reliefweb.int/report/world/human-security-report-2012-sexual-violence-education-and-war-beyond-mainstream; see also Anthony J. Regan, 'Bougainville: Large-Scale Mining and Risks of Conflict Recurrence', *Security Challenges* 10, no. 2 (2014): 72–73, jstor.org/stable/26467882?seq=1.

This book by my friend and colleague Gordon Peake sheds light on the difficulties involved in implementing peace agreements. He recounts, and reflects upon, his own involvement as an external adviser assisting with the implementation of a significant peace agreement – namely, the Bougainville Peace Agreement (the Peace Agreement).

The signing of the long and detailed Peace Agreement in August 2001 concluded a four-year process that ended the nine-year Bougainville conflict (1988–97). It was a complex and violent conflict, involving both a secessionist element – separation of Bougainville from Papua New Guinea (PNG) – and deeply divisive intra-Bougainville violence. The Peace Agreement is regarded by many observers as one of the best and most inclusive of the many peace agreements seeking to resolve territorial intrastate conflicts to have been entered into since the Second World War. That has been the view, for example, of United Nations (UN) officials who were involved, the UN having played a significant role in the negotiation of the Peace Agreement – although not in its implementation.

Gordon was advising on, and seeking to assist in, the development of 'capacity' in the administrative arm of the Autonomous Bougainville Government (ABG): the Bougainville Public Service (since 2014). The ABG was a new subnational government, unique in PNG, established under the Peace Agreement through Bougainville-wide elections held in mid-2005. Gordon's role involved supporting the ABG in the implementation of critically important aspects of the arrangements under the Peace Agreement. These aimed at the ABG gradually achieving a high level of autonomy. This outcome was pursued through a range of measures in the Peace Agreement, many of which had been fully implemented long before Gordon became involved. These measures centred on:

- the enactment of extensive amendments to the PNG Constitution to give effect to the Peace Agreement (completed in March 2002)
- the establishment of the ABG through elections under its own subnational constitution, enacted by a representative Bougainville constituent assembly in accordance with choices made in a long public-consultation process (completed in June 2005)
- protection of ABG autonomy from 'interference' by the PNG government, a goal achieved through elaborate safeguards agreed to in the Peace Agreement and provided for in subsequent amendments to the PNG Constitution and the provisions of the Bougainville Constitution (completed in stages from August 2001 to June 2005).

It was only after the ABG had been established in mid-2005 that efforts could begin with what has been, in retrospect, the most difficult aspect of implementation of the agreed autonomy arrangements. This has involved efforts to add significantly to Bougainville's autonomy through the gradual transfer of an extensive array of functions and powers, many of them significant, from PNG to the ABG. The process became known, during negotiation of the Peace Agreement, as the 'drawdown' of functions and powers. The requirements of the process were spelt out in quite complex arrangements in both the Peace Agreement and PNG constitutional law.

In practice, transfer of the 59 functions and powers enumerated in the PNG Constitution as 'available' for transfer had to be made to a Bougainville public administration that, before the conflict, had met high standards, but which had seen its composition, capacity, morale and accountability standards devastated by the conflict and its aftermath. To complicate matters, the 'drawdown' of particular functions and powers required cooperation from, and joint action with, PNG government agencies. They, too, have demonstrated serious capacity problems, as well as (in some, but not all, cases) resistance to being involved in the process at all.

As a result, the implementation of the autonomy set out in the Peace Agreement has been largely incomplete. Early in 2021, ABG leaders were estimating that only 11 of the 59 'available' functions and powers had been transferred. While, in the Bougainville case, the failure to fully implement autonomy has not resulted in renewed conflict, it has not been without consequence that, from 2005 to 2019, autonomy arrangements did not meet the high expectations held by Bougainvilleans when the Peace Agreement was signed. Undoubtedly, this played a role in the emphatic rejection of the option of 'higher autonomy' offered in the Bougainville independence referendum, held under the terms of the Peace Agreement and the implementing provisions of the PNG Constitution in November–December 2019.[3] In the referendum, 87.4 per cent of enrolled Bougainvilleans cast a vote, and 97.7 per cent of these chose independence, in a ballot in which (unusually for PNG) the electoral roll was remarkably accurate.

---

3   Anthony J. Regan, Kerryn Baker and Thiago Cintra Oppermann, 'The 2019 Bougainville Referendum and the Question of Independence: From Conflict to Consensus', *The Journal of Pacific History* 57, no. 1 (2022): 58–88, doi.org/10.1080/00223344.2021.2010683.

Frustration about the continued slow progress of drawdown has not decreased since Gordon finished working in Bougainville at the end of 2019. The drawdown has been a strong focus of the ABG under President Ishmael Toroama, who was elected in September 2020. In May 2021, he signed, jointly with the PNG government, the Sharp Agreement on the Dispensation of Constitutional Requirements Relating to the Process of Transfer of Functions and Powers. The proposal for this agreement was initiated by the ABG, with the central aim of the ABG doing away with most of the constitutional requirements for the process of transfer. The intention was that the transfer of all functions and powers that had not yet been transferred could be achieved by the end of 2022. In fact, progress since the signing of the Sharp Agreement has been much slower than had been hoped, due, at least in part, to ongoing problems of capacity and focus in both the Bougainville Public Service and the responsible PNG agencies, as illustrated by Gordon's account.

Gordon was part of an ABG-requested, donor-funded effort to implement the 'drawdown' arrangements that were undoubtedly critical to the expected high level of autonomy being achieved, and to develop the capacity of Bougainville Public Service officers to implement these arrangements themselves. When he became involved, the transfer process had already been underway for over 10 years. Gordon had been preceded by at least one other adviser in much the same role, who had struggled to have any impact on the implementation of the drawdown arrangements. Many of those in the ABG and the Bougainville Public Service, who were expected to be key actors in the process, saw little reason to change the status quo.

Gordon's account illustrates the nature of the problems facing an external adviser, and the extent of the difficulty, day to day, of working to implement the wide range of autonomy arrangements commonly found in agreements designed to resolve territorial intrastate conflicts. Such advisers are asked to operate in post-conflict situations, where the capacity of the local state has often been severely undermined by divisive internal conflict, and where the political, historical and cultural contexts can be quite opaque to even the best-read and most engaged external advisers. His account also points to the practical obstacles in the way of external advisers generally (and not just in post-conflict situations) in undertaking activities directed at 'capacity building'.

This is a highly personalised account, quite different from the burgeoning range of analyses of peace agreement implementation written by academics and practitioners. Nevertheless, it sheds real light on the issues discussed in such analyses. Gordon introduces us to some of the wide range of participants in Bougainville's post-conflict rebuilding efforts and seeks to understand why progress in the implementation of key aspects of the Peace Agreement autonomy arrangements has been so limited. His honesty and irony are sometimes confronting, but always illuminating in the light of the realities and challenges involved in trying to ensure that even the best (in terms of content and coverage) peace agreements bear fruit in practice. That can only occur if the challenges of implementing peace agreements are well understood.

Anthony J. Regan
Associate Professor
Department of Pacific Affairs
Coral Bell School of Asia Pacific Affairs
ANU College of Asia and the Pacific
The Australian National University
Canberra

Introduction

Although it was already 10 am, few people were around in the government offices. There was just one beaten-up car in the car park, its door adorned with a sticker bearing the emblem of the Autonomous Bougainville Government (ABG), which features a bulbous headdress called an *upe,* worn by teenage boys during initiation ceremonies in parts of Bougainville. It was my first day in the office. Turning the key, I entered a darkened room, only to be struck by cold as dank and fierce as a sepulchre, thanks to the air conditioner left running full blast for three months – except, that is, for the regular intervals of power outages.

The room looked and smelled like the office of a university don who rarely opened the windows. A few spines of books poked out here and there, but it was the hundreds of orange and yellow manila folders stuffed with papers that commanded my attention. This motley assortment was the handiwork of my predecessor and her predecessor and his predecessor before that, running all the way back to 2005, when this government was established. These uncatalogued papers represented their heritage. Curious, I leafed through them; there were minutes from internal meetings, records of committees, and patchy details referring to working groups and 'technical teams' formed between the Bougainville government and Papua New Guinea (PNG). *What a neat phrase is 'technical teams',* I thought to myself. It conjured up images of furrowed bureaucrats plunging heads down into official records and wrangling over subclauses.

The notes recorded many beginnings but fewer ends; many of the endeavours had petered out after merely a gathering or two. Another feature of the archive was its countless drafts of documents marked 'policy' that aspired to regulate every conceivable governmental endeavour. The documents evoked ardent faith that government could do anything. There was a natural disasters policy in a place where there was no fire brigade, and a hydropower policy for a place in which electricity was intermittent and the grunt-grunt of the diesel generator permeated daily life. Prominent, too, were weighty and sizeable documents bearing important titles such as 'Cocoa value chain study' and 'Coconut husking productivity interim assessment'. Each such document – all paid for by international aid donors – exceeded 250 pages in length, leading me to wonder who would ever have read them. Amid these annals I found a copy of the Egyptian Educational Development Plan 2007–12, bearing the beaming visage of the then president, Hosni Mubarak, and a copy of the national security policy of Jamaica of similar vintage. Inserted within that document was a thin government newsletter from many Christmases ago, talking up projects thought to be about to finish but that years later remained uncompleted.

On top of one flamingo-coloured folder was a bound copy of a Master's thesis[1] written 10 years previously by a man called Raymond Masono. I knew Raymond's name but had yet to meet him. At the time, he was a Master's student at The Australian National University; now, he was one of 14 ministers in the Bougainville government with whom I was to work. In the year after my arrival, he would be appointed vice-president. His thesis, completed long before he joined the government, was written in the style of a man eager to get something off his chest. The abstract read thus:

> While expectations are understandably high, the ABG's ability to meet citizen expectations is being hampered by the government's administrative, institutional and financial capacities, the security situation on the island and a very weak economy. The success or failure of political autonomy, and indeed this post-conflict governance structure, will depend to a large extent on the type of policies that the government designs and implements, as well as its interactions with citizens.[2]

I sat at my desk, hemmed in by this palisade of files, cowed by the efforts of those who had come before me. The air in the room began to feel asphyxiating. I looked up at the walls and saw a solitary poster, its headline proclaiming an 'awareness strategy' and detailing the 'road to the referendum'. As part of the 2001 Bougainville Peace Agreement (the Peace

---

1 Raymond Masono, 'Government Capacity and Citizen Expectations in Bougainville: The Impact of Political Autonomy' (Master's thesis, The Australian National University, 2006), openresearch-repository.anu.edu.au/handle/10440/1142.
2 Masono, 'Government Capacity', 1.

Agreement)[3] that ended the war, Bougainvilleans were granted the right to vote by mid-2020 about their future political status: whether to be independent or remain part of PNG. With the referendum three to four years away, this sleepy office might one day be part of the engine room of the world's newest country. *What did everyone do here?* I wondered, as I looked around, not knowing where to begin. *What did my predecessors leave behind, apart from these files? And what exactly was I doing here?* At that point the room plunged into darkness; the power had cut out again.

* * *

This is a book of travel accounts, histories, vignettes and recollections from four years spent on and off in the Autonomous Region of Bougainville, a place that could, potentially, become the newest country in the world. The period spans the time from my arrival in 2016 to the end of 2019, when Bougainvilleans voted in overwhelming numbers – 97.7 per cent of votes cast – in favour of independence. The manuscript was completed in early 2022, when, notwithstanding the vote's outcome, no flag of an independent Bougainville had yet been raised. Fitful negotiations to give effect to the result have taken place; Bougainville remains an autonomous region of PNG.[4] COVID-19 is an important factor, but it is not the sole one. The difficulty of getting two small and weak bureaucracies – Bougainville and PNG – to knuckle down and develop the administrative nuts and bolts required to give effect to the result is a far weightier factor requiring consideration. Energy levels in both governments pulsate at the drowsy levels they did that humid day when I turned the key to my office door for the first time. It's by no means an exact parallel, but in the four years I worked in Bougainville, leaders in the United Kingdom and the European Union were negotiating the hurdles of Brexit, each with battalions of bureaucrats beavering away in the background. No such battalions do service in this land beyond the Coral Sea, and given that the text of the Brexit withdrawal agreement runs to more than 2,000 pages, the challenge of developing a similar divorce

---

3   'Bougainville Peace Agreement', www.abg.gov.pg/uploads/documents/BOUGAINVILLE_PEACE _AGREEMENT_2001.pdf.

4   Gordon Peake, 'Bougainville's Autonomy Arrangements: Implementation Dilemmas', *The Round Table* 108, no. 3 (2019): 275–92, doi.org/10.1080/00358533.2019.1618610; Anthony J. Regan, 'Autonomy and Conflict Resolution in Bougainville, Papua New Guinea', in *Practising Self-Government: A Comparative Study of Autonomous Regions*, ed. Yash Ghai and Sophia Woodman (Cambridge, UK: Cambridge University Press, 2013), 412–48, doi.org/10.1017/CBO9781139088206.014.

seems insuperable. Another reason for the lack of progress is naked global politics. There are no nation-states in the world that want Bougainville to join their club.

This is in part a scholarly book, in the sense that it carries footnotes and is the product of research. But it also a subjective book, grounded in my own experience, my own mindset and my particular way of seeing the world. It is shaped by a Northern Irish childhood and a career that has toggled between researching and working in parts of the world that once gained headlines for conflict. Others I have worked with would write a much different book about this time, as would Bougainvilleans. I acknowledge that some with an interest in this topic may disagree or have a different interpretation from mine. In 20–25 years, when the cables that diplomats of this time sent back to their capitals are publicly released, we will be able to gain additional insights wrought from the diplomatic frontline, and compare and contrast these with press releases and tweets published at the time. For now, however, this chronicle emerges from my observations and experience, which I hope will shed light on one person's involvement with a time of transition in a place I hold close to my heart and want dearly to see succeed.

Bougainville is a story that reaches beyond this pattern of islands in the Solomon Sea and delves into questions of what is required to become a new addition to the modern map.[5] Bougainville is not the only region seeking to become a country. On the shelf beside my desk as I write sits *An Atlas of Countries That Don't Exist*, which is a book of maps detailing the many regions of the world whose populations are seeking to strike out as independent nations.[6] Among these peoples are the Kurds, the Sahrawis, the people of the English-speaking regions of Cameroon, Tibetans, Assamese, the Moro in the Philippines, Catalans and, closest to Bougainville itself, the Indigenous people of West Papua, which was swallowed by Indonesia in the 1960s.[7] The membership of the Unrepresented Nations and Peoples Organization encompasses more than 50 places and comprises more than 300 million people. By virtue of my Irish Catholicism and many happy years spent living in Timor-

---

5   Roland Paris and Timothy D. Sisk, eds, *The Dilemmas of Statebuilding: Confronting the Contradictions of Postwar Peace Operations* (London & New York: Routledge, 2008).
6   Nick Middleton, *An Atlas of Countries That Don't Exist: A Compendium of Fifty Unrecognized and Largely Unnoticed States* (London: Macmillan, 2015).
7   Pieter Drooglever, *An Act of Free Choice: Decolonisation and the Right to Self-Determination in West Papua* (Oxford: Oneworld, 2009).

Leste, the first new nation of the 21st century, to this day I am drawn instinctively to the romance of nationalist causes and separatism, what the Irish republican leader Ernie O'Malley called 'the singing flame' of independence.[8] Bougainville, however, taught me just how difficult it is to run a government and to source the skills required to do so properly. Fancy titles such as 'technical teams' may make for a spectacle of administration, but they achieve little else.

Engaging with Bougainville and places like it is a challenge for the fluid concept that is 'the international community'.[9] For decades, scholars and researchers have been wrestling with the question of how to effectively support societies emerging from conflict[10] and in places where the reach of government does not extend much beyond the door of the office. A large cottage industry of think tanks and academics is working on the topic. It is impossible to keep up; the paper produced daily could match the amount I found amassed in my Bougainville office. Yet, just as in Timor-Leste, I found there is a major gap between, on the one hand, strategy and thought on paper, and on the other, real-world policy in action, in part because many of the people who do the writing do not do the work of implementation.

A feature of many such places is that efforts are made to build effective administrations in places with no previous history of them. Writing specifically about peace agreements (although their findings have broader application), Ashraf Ghani and Clare Lockhart find a general lack of focus in the literature about who is to do the work.[11] They write that a 'leitmotif running through [peace agreements] is the need for a state apparatus that is professionally staffed, capable, honest, and infused with the value of public service', but that little attention is paid to how to attain that goal.[12]

8   Ernie O'Malley, *The Singing Flame* (Dublin: Anvil Books, 1992).
9   Berit Bliesemann de Guevara and Florian P. Kühn, '"The International Community Needs to Act": Loose Use and Empty Signalling of a Hackneyed Concept', *International Peacekeeping* 18, no. 2 (2011): 135–51, doi.org/10.1080/13533312.2011.546082; Bruno Simma and Andreas L. Paulus, 'The "International Community": Facing the Challenge of Globalization', *European Journal of International Law* 9, no. 2 (1998): 266–77, doi.org/10.1093/ejil/9.2.266.
10   Mary B. Anderson, *Do No Harm: How Aid Can Support Peace – or War* (Boulder, CO: Lynne Rienner Publishers, 1999).
11   Ashraf Ghani and Clare Lockhart, *Fixing Failed States: A Framework for Rebuilding a Fractured World* (Oxford: Oxford University Press, 2007).
12   Ashraf Ghani and Clare Lockhart, 'Writing the History of the Future: Securing Stability through Peace Agreements', *Journal of Intervention and Statebuilding* 1, no. 3 (2007): 284, doi.org/10.1080/17502970701592249.

Few places emerging from conflict have a public service able to correspond to such a functioning image, something that Ashraf Ghani in particular knows only too well. He was president of Afghanistan from 2014 to 2021 before fleeing the Taliban's march on Kabul. His doomed efforts when in the top job illustrate the gulf between opining about *how* things should be done and actually doing something about them.

Moreover, this academic or policy-oriented style of writing – sober, deliberative, logical, solution-oriented – is not a natural fit for many of the challenges I found in Bougainville, or indeed anywhere. One crucial challenge is that in many ways the implementation of the prescribed activity is an innately human endeavour, one marked by human foibles. Yet, the role of individuals – the good, the bad; the hard-working, the shirking; the committed, the crack-brained – is missing entirely from the writing about it, in defiance of reality. In Bougainville, as everywhere, individuals are intensely visible to one another, their strengths, quirks and idiosyncrasies gabbed about at length. In not writing about them, we show cognitive dissonance about the importance of human agency.

It's not just Bougainville. While the project I worked on was funded by Australian aid, the challenges I encountered are the same no matter who is stumping up. The cookbook for such places is filled with familiar recipes irrespective of location: the deployment of technical advisers to support nascent governments, grants to boost agriculture and stimulate the economy, money to build roads, support for rural areas, and support for broad goals like 'governance', 'justice' and 'public administration'. There is an obsession with not deviating from the ingredients list; many aid projects are characterised by long-range and weighty plans developed years in advance. Forceful emphasis is placed upon reporting that every recipe has resulted in the production of a triumphant dish; for example, researchers found that 96 per cent of Australia's official words about its own aid program are positive.[13] Few people working at the coalface believe in the veracity of this figure, yet the seeming reluctance to publicly acknowledge harder truths about the difficulty of this line of work is pervasive.

---

13   David Green and Kaisha Crupi, 'Public Aid Performance Reporting: Could Less Be Better?', *Devpolicy* (blog), 30 June 2020, devpolicy.org/public-aid-performance-reporting-could-less-be-better-20200630-2/.

Typing the last paragraph triggered a memory, of a beachfront banquet in Dili, the capital of Timor-Leste, held one sultry, windless night many years ago, at a time when the most recent Nokia phone was still the status symbol. The dinner was held in honour of a visiting Australian minister, there on a flying visit. The minister looked bored by the stilted chatter. When it was suggested everyone switch seats after dinner to enliven the deadening atmosphere, I was just heading off to the bathroom, and I returned to find the minister sitting alone. Having nowhere else to go, I plonked myself down next to him. We had a great chat. We spoke about this and that – our shared love of cricket, his Irish heritage, the liminal delights of high-status Qantas lounges, a tip on public speaking that I use to this day (grip a pen tightly). Then he turned to me and said: 'Can you tell me if this project is working well, because I don't believe all these long reports I'm being given. They read like boring fairy stories.' Thereupon, the minister's staffers decided it was high time the meeting concluded.

I believe it is fundamental that we tell more than a boring fairy story; instead, we need to hear a more adult, less utopian, more dappled tale. Although scribes abound within the fields of post-conflict reconstruction and aid, individuals with most of the accumulated knowledge about the ironies, absurdities, contradictions and Sisyphean challenges of such work rarely describe their experiences, whether in books, academic tomes or, indeed, anywhere else. That's understandable. This is a precarious and uncertain line of work; when I worked as a consultant I didn't get paid for these assignments until the product – invariably a report – was accepted, a remuneration arrangement that always concentrated the mind. We need to acknowledge that this is difficult work, and the unalloyed success of activities aimed at assisting in transitions to statehood is the exception rather than the norm.[14] In this book, I touch on the good work that aid is achieving in complicated and difficult settings. If there is a moral and a wider application to my tale, it is to be found in an appeal for humility, and for more realistic thinking about the possibilities and inherent limitations of such assistance, with less of a focus on convincing people that everything is tickety-boo.

---

14   Oliver P. Richmond, *Failed Statebuilding: Intervention, the State, and the Dynamics of Peace Formation* (New Haven and London: Yale University Press, 2014), doi.org/10.12987/yale/97803 00175318.001.0001.

PART ONE

*Reformers have the idea that change can be achieved
by brute sanity alone.*

— George Bernard Shaw

1

Aid comes to my aid

Many tales of people who came to be in PNG for long stints begin with a tale of flight. This, was how I, too, found myself in Bougainville, although my story is not as romantic, radical or tragic as the stories of some who came to these islands before me. I hadn't fathered a child with someone I shouldn't; I wasn't fleeing the long arm of tax authorities or judgement by a bankruptcy court. I hadn't come to find Utopia, as had the German August Engelhardt[1] and his followers, cocovores who lived (and died) solely on coconuts just before the Great War; or the hundreds of French, Belgian and Spanish colonists induced by the Marquis de Rays[2] to move from Europe to 'La Nouvelle France', a new empire he created on a malarial coast. I wasn't like Errol Flynn,[3] who came seeking a fortune. Nor was I discovered there by a Hollywood talent scout while brawling with a crocodile, as he was. But I was fleeing all the same.

I arrived via the most unusual route: the Republic of Zimbabwe. My wife Suzanne – I love her with all my heart – is a diplomat, and we moved there for her job. It quickly turned into a disaster. We hadn't thought too hard about the decision before going there. It sounded like a great family adventure, and some previous leaps in the dark, such as moving on a whim to Timor-Leste, had worked out spectacularly well. That was where

---

1   Nina Martyris, 'Death By Coconut: A Story of Food Obsession Gone Too Far', NPR, 3 December 2015, npr.org/sections/thesalt/2015/12/03/457124796/death-by-coconut-a-story-of-food-obsession-gone-too-far.
2   Bill Metcalf, 'Utopian Fraud: The Marquis de Rays and La Nouvelle-France', *Utopian Studies* 22, no. 1 (2011): 104–24, doi.org/10.1353/utp.2011.0014.
3   Patricia O'Brien, 'Wild Colonial Boy: Errol Flynn's Rape Trial, Pacific Pasts and the Making of Hollywood', *Australian Historical Studies* 52, no. 4 (2021): 591–610, doi.org/10.1080/1031461X.2021.1889006.

we met, and without that place, without taking that chance, we would never have found each other and created two wonderful sons, Charles and Patrick. However, I was totally unprepared for what I encountered in Harare. Being a 'plus one' in a privileged cocoon inside an impoverished and unhappy country was unquestionably the hardest job I have ever had. Hardest of all was that my role meant I felt obliged to keep what in Papua New Guinean pidgin (Tok Pisin) is called 'pasim maus', a shut mouth, which is something I've never been very good at. For many of the people we met in the diplomatic bubble, the conventions of the profession meant inoculation against speaking what was plainly obvious to anyone who could see what was right in front of them. The state was a venal, inept and occasionally murderous racket,[4] but conventions of diplomacy meant that for plenipotentiaries of other states, what mattered most was to forge relationships with the people within it. One ambassador was particularly one-eyed, discerning winds of change in a place where the air did not circulate. I was frustrated, bored, crabby, at endless loose ends, and after a few months the only thing lowering faster than my golf handicap was my sense of self-worth. I saw clearly then why some of the spouses I'd met in both Dili and various diplomatic outposts across the Pacific looked permanently frayed and unhappy. Another diplomatic family left hastily; the rumour went around that the desolate spouse had threatened the chef with a carving knife.

Then a solution seemed to present itself – a job advertisement for a position in the Autonomous Region of Bougainville, which was possibly as far from Zimbabwe as one could imagine. The preamble to the job description was enticing, written with an urgent and dignified tone:

> The Bougainville Peace Agreement, and various associated Constitutional and Organic laws, commit the two Governments to cooperate towards implementing autonomy arrangements. Specifically, the legal framework provides for a transfer of listed functions and powers to the ABG, in close collaboration with the National Government, to ensure the ABG has sufficient capacity, assets and finance to implement the transferred powers and functions.

---

4   Peter Godwin, *The Fear: The Last Days of Robert Mugabe* (London and Oxford: Picador, 2010); Christina Lamb, *House of Stone: The True Story of a Family Divided in War-Torn Zimbabwe* (London: Harper Perennial, 2007); Douglas Rogers, *The Last Resort: A Memoir of Mischief and Mayhem on a Family Farm in Africa* (New York: Three Rivers Press, 2009).

Recent Joint Supervisory Board meetings have agreed [on] the need for a more proactive approach to [the] transfer of powers, including the establishment of a proposed overarching Memorandum of Understanding (MoU) between the Governments. The MoU elaborates the draw-down process and obligations of each government. It is intended to facilitate accelerated draw-down and closer intergovernmental cooperation.[5]

The role entailed helping to nudge this process along. The job formed part of a program of Australian support, and the successful candidate, if the job description was to be read at face value, would be helming important and innovative work. It sounded more alluring than another round of golf and seemed the perfect opportunity to deploy experiences of doing something similar in previous jobs and academic research.

I knew the place, to an extent. I'd been to Bougainville a couple of times for short stints, the last of these in 2012, when I had conducted a review of a community policing program.[6]

On that occasion, my fellow consultant and I had spent a few days in the tumbledown administrative capital, Buka, and my memory was of how small but how fabulously adorned in titles the government had seemed, and how sparsely peopled. Now, the only person in the office of the president was the leader himself.

The president was John Momis, a storied figure in the political history of both Bougainville and PNG, a personification of its intertwinements and frays. He was born in 1942 to a father from an 'important chiefly clan'[7] in Buin, in Bougainville's south, and a mother of Chinese and New Ireland descent. His father's cousin was Papala, an opponent of the German colonial powers that once ruled Bougainville. In Momis's own words, penned in a chapter of a book about Bougainville prior to the conflict, Papala:

5   Autonomous Bougainville Government, *Terms of Reference: Facilitator: ABG Draw Down of Powers and Functions*, 2015, secure.dc2.pageuppeople.com/apply/TransferRichTextFile.ashx?sData=Fwg6i4 Eli-CoeHxcf6yljYD2wQX1rxvDU5b4AFSzHGBNw_RJmty7rxCQJvvAjmCRkbP6c8CRcC4~.

6   Sinclair Dinnen and Gordon Peake, *Bougainville Community Policing Project: Independent Evaluation* (New Zealand Ministry of Foreign Affairs and Trade, February 2013), mfat.govt.nz/ assets/Aid-Prog-docs/Evaluations/2013/Feb-2013/Bougainville-Commuity-Policing-Project-BCPP-Independent-Evaluation-February-2013-Public-Version.pdf.

7   John Lawrence Momis, 'Shaping Leadership through Bougainville Indigenous Values and Catholic Seminary Training – A Personal Journey', in *Bougainville before the Conflict*, ed. Anthony J. Regan and Helga M. Griffin (Canberra: ANU Press, 2015), 300–16, doi.org/10.22459/BBC.08.2015.

ordered his soldiers to kill the paramount *luluai* [administration-appointed local chief], policemen and catechist … because he saw them as agents of the foreign powers seeking to impose their authority with its corruptive influences.[8]

Momis had similar goals to those of his forefather – self-determination for both the individual and the nation – but took a diametrically different path, one that was shaped by, among other things, Catholic social teaching and his study of the experiences of Martin Luther King Jr. A seminarian and ordained priest, he went into politics and joined fellow young Papua New Guinean leaders seeking to unshackle themselves from Australian colonial rule. Elected as a member for Bougainville, he led the Constitutional Planning Commission between 1972 and 1974 that helped write Papua New Guinea's constitution, resigning shortly before independence was due to be granted in 1975 on the grounds that Bougainville was not receiving a fair allocation of responsibilities and revenue within the new state. He co-signed a petition to the United Nations to lobby against the granting of Papua New Guinea's independence before the status of Bougainville was resolved and travelled to New York to make the case, the journey paid out of a pool of monies collected throughout Bougainville. 'Should the United Nations fail to properly discharge its duties of protecting our interests, we will be left with no alternative but to secede unilaterally from Papua New Guinea,'[9] he wrote in a letter, giving his address as c/o the Waldorf Astoria Hotel. They left empty-handed. A year later Momis forged a compromise arrangement whereby Bougainville would receive provincial autonomy within the newly independent state of Papua New Guinea.

Momis went on to occupy many of the high offices of state. He was responsible for decentralisation and was Papua New Guinea's ambassador to China. He has an honorary doctorate from The Papua New Guinea University of Technology. Momis was a negotiator and co-signatory of the Bougainville Peace Agreement in 2001 and was elected president of the region in 2010. On the day we met him, he was wearing an unprepossessing beige safari suit suggestive of his radical beginnings.

8   Momis, 'Shaping Leadership', 301.
9   John Lawrence Momis, 'Petition from Father John Momis and Mr. John Teosin Concerning the Trust Territory of New Guinea', *United Nations Digital Library*, digitallibrary.un.org/record/3823491?ln=en.

The very thinly peopled office seemed an apt metaphor for the state of Bougainville. Architects – Momis among them – had helped fashion the structures, but there was still much work to be done to animate them.

Most of our time on this 2012 visit was spent outside Buka, on the eponymous island of Bougainville. We'd juddered our way on scrabbled dust roads in a Land Cruiser driven by an ex-combatant from the Bougainville Revolutionary Army (BRA)[10] called Lowell, a man with a musculature so cut that he could have won a body-building competition. As a young man, Lowell had fought in the 1988–97 conflict[11] – what people referred to as 'the Crisis' – and now was working as a PMV driver, the abbreviation standing for 'public motor vehicle', a shared taxi that shuttled passengers between the old capital of Arawa and Kokopau, a sprawling town at the tip of the main island of Bougainville. From there it was a short boat ride over to Buka. In church halls we interviewed anyone we could get our hands on, resting on wooden benches shaded under the boughs of large trees.

My abiding memory of the visit was how so many people we met had metabolised fully all the high modernist syntax and argot of governance and aid: they spoke about frameworks, modalities, projects, crosscutting issues and technical teams as fluently as any consultant. In a police station in Buin, a town in the south of Bougainville, the cellophane remained intact on leather chairs and desks more than 10 years after they had been delivered, giving the station the feel of a beached *Mary Celeste*. Australia had delivered the office equipment in advance of a deployment of its Federal Police, who, because of a legal dispute, were never to come.[12]

---

10   Mike Forster, 'The Bougainville Revolutionary Army', *The Contemporary Pacific* 4, no. 2 (1992): 368–72, jstor.org/stable/23699905.
11   For a more detailed overview of the conflict and peace process, see, for example, John Braithwaite et al., *Reconciliation and Architectures of Commitment: Sequencing Peace in Bougainville* (Canberra: ANU E Press, 2010); Colin Filer, 'The Bougainville Rebellion, the Mining Industry and the Process of Social Disintegration in Papua New Guinea', *Canberra Anthropology* 13, no. 1 (1990): 1–39, doi.org/10.1080/03149099009508487; Eugene Ogan, 'The Bougainville Conflict: Perspectives from Nasioi', *State Society and Governance in Melanesia Discussion Paper* 99, no. 3 (1999), openresearch-repository.anu.edu.au/bitstream/1885/41820/3/ssgmogan99-3.pdf; Anthony J. Regan, 'Causes and Course of the Bougainville Conflict', *Journal of Pacific History* 33, no. 3 (1998): 269–85, doi.org/10.1080/00223349808572878.
12   Abby McLeod and Sinclair Dinnen, 'Police Building in the Southwest Pacific – New Directions in Australian Regional Policing', in *Crafting Transnational Policing: Police Capacity-Building and Global Policing Reform*, ed. Andrew Goldsmith and James Sheptycki (Oxford and Portland: Hart Publishing, 2007), 295–328.

Inside the station a police officer told us that he needed 'training'. 'Training in what?' we asked him. 'Training in capacity building,' he replied, plucking effortlessly another term from the development lexicon. Ideally in Port Moresby. Preferably at a hotel. Lasting for at least a week; a fortnight would be even better. He didn't appear too vexed as to what the training would be about, or its value; he simply wanted to get away for a little bit. I admired his candour.

In Port Moresby on the way out, we met first with some junior diplomats funding the trip to brief them on our findings. 'Something must be done,' one thundered, and maybe then I might have believed her. After that, we went to meet the director of the National Coordination Office for Bougainville Affairs (NCOBA) in Port Moresby, the office of the PNG government responsible for synchronising government support to the region. It was a funereally quiet place the day we visited. The workforce consisted of a few people staring into space; someone was playing solitaire on his old computer.

A senior official nodded vigorously as we recited our earnest findings and suggested that we call a 'strategy meeting' to discuss the issue further – in Honiara, capital of nearby Solomon Islands – and preferably in a nice hotel. For at least a week, but a fortnight would be better.

In the years since that trip, I had returned reasonably often to Port Moresby, writing technical reports for various arms of aid programs: plans, reviews, designs. Aid is a wordy business, and I felt betimes like a railway stoker, shovelling words into the bureaucratic furnace to keep it chugging to the next station. Of an evening at the Holiday Inn, a hotel popular with the development set, I'd share drinks with expatriate government advisers making light work of the house red and speaking about what I was semaphoring in all my reports as a 'challenging delivery context'. Their nightly shoptalk was absenteeism in offices, intermittent electricity supply, workshops unfailingly starting a few hours late, passive resistance and the resigned resentments encountered daily.

There was a timeless and familiar quality to such grievances. The academic literature about government in Melanesia[13] makes for miserable reading: it portrays the organisations we were working with as slapdash, pedantic, dilatory and inattentive. Writing in 2006, the historian Hank Nelson observed:

---

13   Ron May, ed., *Policy Making and Implementation: Studies from Papua New Guinea* (Canberra: ANU E Press, 2009), doi.org/10.22459/PMI.09.2009.

> Given the inability of many government departments and agencies
> to carry out basic functions – such as keep files on employees and
> pay and promote them – there is not much point expecting them
> to implement [anything] major.[14]

A few years later, Mark Turner and David Kavanamur wrote about the
bureaucracy's 'incremental decay rendering it inappropriate for the tasks
it is supposed to perform'.[15] The US government, in a cable leaked by
Wikileaks, characterised the government of PNG as a 'dysfunctional
blob'.[16] After his visits to PNG, Francis Fukuyama put it this way: 'For any
given reform, donors have to be realistic about their potential leverage and
work within the constraints given by the political system.' He went on
to say that 'the political context cannot be abolished or wished away'.[17]
The trouble, of course, is that admitting to such problems is difficult
for the donors who support all this activity, and hard for scribes like me
to put into the official record without getting thwacked. This may well
explain why there is a growing turn in the literature – both aid memoir
and academic writing – to peer behind the bureaucratic curtain, reflect
on challenges and state more baldly the structural, political and practical
challenges of implementation. Often these books are written as narrative.
This book fits within this literature.[18]

The genre of reports on development projects offered no reward for
producing a draft with a well-turned phrase, vivid character portrait
or punchy sentence. I learned my lessons the hard way during this time,
when a draft was returned to me with the comment that it read like an
article from *Newsweek*. In my naivety, I initially thought the remark

14   Hank Nelson, 'Governments, States and Labels', *State Society and Governance in Melanesia Discussion Paper* 6 (2006): 17, openresearch-repository.anu.edu.au/bitstream/1885/10134/1/Nelson_GovernmentsStates2006.pdf.

15   Mark Turner and David Kavanamur, 'Explaining Public Sector Reform Failure: Papua New Guinea 1975–2001', in *Policy Making and Implementation: Studies from Papua New Guinea*, ed. Ron May (Canberra: ANU E Press, 2009), 9–25, 21, doi.org/10.22459/PMI.09.2009.02.

16   Philip Dorling, 'PNG Exposed as "Dysfunctional Blob"', *The Sydney Morning Herald*, 4 September 2011, smh.com.au/world/png-exposed-as-dysfunctional-blob-20110903-1jrcx.html.

17   Francis Fukuyama, *Governance Reform in Papua New Guinea* (World Bank Document, 2017), 4 and 13, documents1.worldbank.org/curated/en/426851468145477761/pdf/686490ESW0P11400in0Papua0New0Guinea.pdf.

18   See, for example, Robert E. Klitgaard, *Tropical Gangsters: One Man's Experience with Development and Decadence in Deepest Africa* (New York: Basic Books, 1990); Inez Baranay, *Rascal Rain: A Year in Papua New Guinea* (Sydney: HarperCollins Imprint, 1994); Séverine Autesserre, *Peaceland: Conflict Resolution and the Everyday Politics of International Intervention* (Cambridge: Cambridge University Press, 2014); Tom Bamforth, *Deep Field: Dispatches from the Frontlines of Aid Relief* (Richmond, Victoria: Hardie Grant Books, 2014).

was intended as high praise. Few were interested in recitations of more complex, nuanced and human truths, such as the long shadows of colonialism or a political system focused on resource acquisition for the clan or tribe. The officials administering the aid would admit as much after turning around to check the coast was clear, but publicly querying the efficacy of these efforts was a step too far. There was the occasional bit of mordant humour to be had, such as when I found a giant oven outside the side entrance to the 'Centre of Excellence' of the Royal Papua New Guinea Constabulary; whoever had ordered it some years earlier had not measured its dimensions against those of the narrow door it needed to fit through, and now it was serving as a makeshift cupboard. The oven reminded me of a line from Shelley's poem *Ozymandias*: 'Look on my Works, ye Mighty, and despair!'[19] For the most part, this was trying work that I took on largely because doing it bought me the time I needed to finish my book on Timor-Leste.[20]

Hence, when we left for Zimbabwe, the last thing on my mind was a return to Bougainville, PNG, or even the aid business, but a year of kicking my heels caused a volte-face. Suddenly, the profession I had been happy to get shot of seemed deeply alluring. I was surprised at the extent to which the job description was brimming with vim but prepared to suspend incredulity if it aided the cause of getting me out of here. I applied for the job, was interviewed, shouted my answers down a rickety phone connection and was as surprised as all get-out to find I was successful. I told the spouse of the British ambassador that I was going to PNG. He heard the 'N' as 'and' and wished me well in my position with the pharmaceutical company Proctor and Gamble.

So, just after Christmas, I found myself on a flight path from Harare to Johannesburg to Sydney to Port Moresby. I was put in the old Holiday Inn for a few days, where little seemed to have changed in the intervening years, not even the menu. The beef rendang was still spiceless and the red wine as lukewarm as it used to be. Running machines at the broiling gym continued to test agility and dexterity by switching off without warning, and the worn sign that proclaimed, 'New equipment coming soon' had been there since that first visit in 2012. There was still a dedicated line

19   Percy Bysshe Shelley, '*P B Shelley "Ozymandias" 1817*', British Library, bl.uk/learning/timeline/item126940.html.
20   Gordon Peake, *Beloved Land: Stories, Struggles and Secrets from Timor-Leste* (Melbourne: Scribe 2013).

item for safari suits on the laundry list. The stories in the two daily newspapers – the *Post Courier* and *The National* – were facsimiles of those published years before: police chiefs were finger-wagging about the need for law and order, while political leaders were making thundering announcements or launching new fix-it-all schemes. A page in both newspapers was dedicated to Bougainville, and the stories were similar: eulogies to training programs recently finished, paeans to corporate plans, and announcements that new gender and social inclusion strategies were being launched. Of the commitment to draw down governmental powers *post-haste*[21] that was the basis of my ostensible job there was no mention.

I called in at the NCOBA office, which was now in a different location, adjacent to a Chinese seafood restaurant a block away from the city's brewery. I remember Suzanne calling me as I arrived, and my telling her where I was. I spoke about the role of the office. 'Oh, that sounds very grand,' she said. I switched the call into video mode to show the scene before me: a large meeting room, three quarters of which was filled with a table of walnut veneer and no-one sitting on the well-appointed leather chairs. The office pinboard was filled with clippings heralding historical signing ceremonies and commitments to 'work around the clock' for peace. There was a new director in charge, but I could not detect a lot of energy in the office this time around, either. I recognised the solitaire player from years earlier, mesmerised this time by the blue-fringed page of Facebook. I was expecting to be grilled about my plans for the job, but there were no such questions; the director asked for an upgrade to the office internet on the grounds that this would improve productivity. I uttered something non-committal; his request brought to my mind earlier times when every application to an aid donor in Timor-Leste included a line item for a sound system. Why couldn't we just admit that one reason why the aid program we were part of was smiled at and tolerated was that one might get lucky on an equipment tombola?

---

21   Joint Supervisory Body, 'Joint Review of Bougainville's Autonomy Arrangements by Government of Papua New Guinea and the Autonomous Government of Bougainville', 23 October 2013, bougainvillenews.files.wordpress.com/2015/03/joint-review-of-autonomy-arrangements-jsb-and-rc-approved-joint-resolutions.pdf.

2

Arrival

I spent a few happily humdrum days in Port Moresby before catching the 9 am flight to Buka, where my job would be based. The journey took less than two hours, the in-flight snack comprising two fondant chocolate biscuits and a little cup of orange juice. The plane landed shortly after midday. Coasting on our approach over an opalescent reef, we landed smoothly, and a red tractor with flashing lights directed the plane to the small terminal. 'Please adjust your watches to Bougainville time,' the pilot said, intoning words of welcome on the tannoy while we disembarked. The pilot's reminder related to the job I was expected to do. As part of the Peace Agreement, Bougainville's government was entitled to 'draw down' a number of governmental powers and functions,[1] and my job was to chivvy this process along. Thus far, one of the few powers they'd managed to draw down was the power to change the time zone. The Autonomous Region of Bougainville was one hour ahead of the rest of PNG and in the same time zone as neighbouring Solomon Islands. I adjusted my wind-up watch, but my iPhone did not automatically update; Digicel, the mobile phone company, had not yet changed its systems to reflect the new time zone. By then the 'new' time zone had been in place for more than five years.

The airport had altered little in the years since my last visit, and I remembered the old artillery gun from the Second World War near the perimeter, still pointing menacingly up into the sky as if waiting for a ghost Japanese kamikaze. The other new arrivals and I walked into a little

---

1   Kylie McKenna, *Implementation of the Bougainville Peace Agreement: Implications for Referendum*, PNG National Research Institute Research Report 6 (2019), 7–12.

tin-roofed waiting area separated from the rest of the terminal by a metal grille that reminded me of a church confessional. There we waited for our bags to be loaded onto a tractor trailer and dumped just outside the door, whereupon an almighty scramble ensued to be the first person to locate luggage, re-enter the waiting area and skedaddle out through another door. This fracas made me recall going to mass with my family in my childhood, and how my father could never understand why so many people would clamber and jostle in the queue for communion the moment the priest came down from the altar. He always made us wait until the end, and I adopted his sensible, measured approach in Buka, being the last person out of the terminal, where a security guard at the exit was ensuring that the baggage tags matched the receipt. Dressed in sandy combat fatigues, the guard appeared primed for desert warfare; his uniform bore the badge of the High Risk Security Company. Each time I passed in and out of this airport in the following years, I thought how peculiar it was for a business in the provision of security to characterise its services this way.

Standing beside a weathered old public information billboard warning about the dangers of AIDS, a woman named Maria and a driver called Willie were waiting for me outside. Both of them were local staff working on the program. Maria had a clipboard with one page on it, which, I could see, had lots of boxes on the right. 'We are going to take you on a familiarisation drive of Buka and surroundings,' she said, full of well-meaning officiousness. I had remembered Buka as small with a handful of streets. *Perhaps it had expanded significantly in the few years since I'd been there?*

After a thoroughgoing 15-minute tour, I knew for certain that the town had changed little. There was the port, and beside it the copra mill; a bakery; a couple of hotels; some second-hand clothing stores, and a bank with a hundreds-deep scrum of people waiting to use its two ATMs (automated teller machines). The largest structure in town was still the same: a bustling open-air market with a greying shingle roof, where Bougainvillean women sold their fruit and vegetables. The betel nut market still thrived beside it, and not far away was the boat stop for the trip over to the larger Bougainville island. We passed a petrol station, where fuel was being manually pumped into a car from one of several giant red drums, then past a patch of green the size of a soccer penalty-box with a bandstand to one side and stalls selling death-metal T-shirts. This was Bel Isi ('Peace') Park, and it was the smallest park I had ever seen. From there, we drove out of town for five minutes, past the airport, and Maria showed us the parliament and presidential offices. Neither had any cars parked beside them.

We drove past the government offices; Maria pointed to where I had worked in the past. 'But no-one's there now,' she said, matter-of-factly. 'Lunchtime. Come back around two-thirty.' I ticked and initialled the 14 boxes on her clipboard, attesting that I had completed the grand tour, and was dropped at one of the town's handful of hotel-restaurants, Reasons Bar & Grill.

As I walked up the wooden steps, I looked down and noticed a large pizza oven sitting in the corner below, presumably because it was too heavy to lug up the stairs. I was reminded of the 'centre of excellence'. Upstairs, I met one of my new colleagues, an Australian lawyer called John, who both looked and dressed like Johnny Cash in his later years and carried the knowing air of the old island hand. I ordered fish soup, which came with little finger slices of buttered bread. Our table looked out onto the waterway of the Buka passage, where motorised banana boats were scooting back and forth, while wooden canoes followed the direction of the tide. John had googled me, so he knew I'd been in Timor-Leste. 'Never been there, always wanted to go, and I'd imagined Bougainville would be like that when I came here: a place where an energetic nation-building project would be underway. I wasn't expecting it to be as slow as it is.' I inquired about the 'drawdown of powers' process that, as per my job description, was being prioritised. The process had stalled somewhat. In the time between the job advertisement and my interview, the chief secretary, who was head of the public service, had been suspended on charges of financial chicanery, and a temporary incumbent was in place who was spending a lot of his time away in Port Moresby. (Both men would ultimately be dismissed from their posts.)

John dropped me at the project office, located on the second floor of a building that housed the Department of Treasury and Finance, which, when I arrived, had a total of two people inside. The project office upstairs was a much more crowded affair, 20 or so people jammed together, hunched over laptops. A few expatriates sat among this crowd, but most of the staff were either from Bougainville or elsewhere in PNG.

It all felt very first-day-at-school, but, improbably, it was my mentioning I'd come from Zimbabwe that broke the awkwardness. 'Do Zimbabweans love telling Mugabe jokes, too?' one asked. *What?* It turned out the old tyrant had quite a following here, courtesy of oddball sayings (mistakenly) attributed to him, shared, liked and commented upon through social media. The memes presented Mugabe as a lovable old rascal with a capacity for knowing asides and sly humour, a characterisation that would have surprised many of the 14 million Zimbabweans labouring under his 'kakistocracy' – a word I learned in Harare to describe the rule of the most venal and incompetent.

I talked about the time we met the old leader and how distinctly non-gregarious but fascinating he was. We met at State House in Harare, once home to the colonial governors, where we had gone so that Suzanne could present her diplomatic credentials. On the walls were pastoral scenes of fox-hunting and hounds in English dales, and on the tables, tea and oozing cream puffs were served on Wedgewood china. Mugabe didn't want to talk politics or opine on the dismal state of his country; he wanted to palaver about the cricket, recite poetry and moan about how Australia was denying him an entry visa. What surprised me most about Zimbabwe was how much this country reminded me of an England of long ago. I'd gone expecting revolutionary fervency and instead found a colonial time capsule, a state that seemed to exist purely for the purposes of aggrandising the people in charge. 'Zimbabwe sounds a bit like Papua New Guinea,' said a man who introduced himself as George. 'We've kept so much of the old Australia here, too,' he said. I'd never really thought about that before – but he was right.

George was from Central Province in PNG, a man in his sixties with a scrum half's build, a thick mop of black hair and a pair of bifocal glasses. He was to become one of my closest and dearest friends. A former public servant in Port Moresby, he was now a 'Human Resources' adviser to the Bougainville government. There were 10–15 such advisers working within the government who rotated in and out; my arrival meant there was now another. The advisory model is a ubiquitous feature of many development projects. Every year a quarter of international aid – approximately US$15 billion globally – is spent on capacity development.[2]

---

2   Matthew Andrews et al., 'The Challenge of Building (Real) State Capability', Harvard Kennedy School Working Paper 74 (2015), papers.ssrn.com/sol3/papers.cfm?abstract_id=2700331; Volker Boege et al., 'On Hybrid Political Orders and Emerging States: What Is Failing – States in the Global South or Research and Politics in the West?', Berghof Handbook Dialogue Series 8 (2009): 15–35; Derick W. Brinkerhoff and Jennifer M. Brinkerhoff, 'Public Sector Management Reform in Developing Countries: Perspectives Beyond NPM Orthodoxy', *Public Administration and Development* 35, no. 4 (2015): 222–37, doi.org/10.1002/pad.1739; Lisa Denney and R. Mallett with M.S. Benson, 'Service Delivery and State Capacity: Findings from the Secure Livelihoods Research Consortium, London', securelivelihoods. org/wp-content/uploads/Service-delivery-and-state-capacity_Findings-from-the-Secure-Livelihoods-Research-Consortium.pdf; James Ferguson, *The Anti-Politics Machine: Development, Depoliticization, and Bureaucratic Power in Lesotho* (Minneapolis, MN: University of Minnesota Press, 1994); Mary Venner, 'The Concept of "Capacity" in Development Assistance: New Paradigm or More of the Same?', *Global Change, Peace & Security* 27, no. 1 (2015): 85–96, doi.org/10.1080/14781158.2015.994488.

The theory is nearly as old as the hills, and it goes like this: parts of government (and the individuals forming it) lack the capacity required to discharge responsibilities effectively and require 'capacity building' to be able to do so. The role of the adviser is to serve as a cross between motivational coach, knowledgeable professor, repository of ideas, modeler of appropriate bureaucratic behaviour and shoulder to cry on. It is one of the omnipresent features of aid delivery, but as yet no agreed coherent, effective way to monitor and evaluate it has been developed to determine whether it does any good at all. The role of adviser attracts all kinds of different people and groups, each invested in evangelising the people they visit in the different approaches they think might be effective. Yet, various incentives are at play that cloud the formation of objective judgement: the donors who pay for the work are skittish about generating newspaper headlines, and the individuals who work as advisers have multiple, mixed incentives, as do the people they are working with. I've worked with some brilliant technical advisers and those at the at the other end of the spectrum.

A huge library of material[3] – I have contributed to it myself with my numerous windy reports – has been built up, in an attempt to winkle out and explicate what advisers do, for the purpose of assigning some measurable value to that work.[4] Part of the problem is that technical advisers are visible – especially in Bougainville, where my skin differs so evidently in colour from the burnished black skin of many around me – but what they try to accomplish is not. Advice and ideas cannot be seen. Advising can support. It can facilitate. It can try to spark. By its very nature, however, it produces nothing on its own that can be sustainable. It can only stand a chance of being effective when paired with something else, just as a matchstick requires a striking strip, a coffee needs a cup, or the door to my office needed a key.

3   Andrews et al., 'Challenge', 74; Boege et al., 'Hybrid Political Orders'; Brinkerhoff and Brinkerhoff, 'Public Sector Management'; Derick Brinkerhoff and Peter Morgan, 'Capacity and Capacity Development: Coping with Complexity', *Public Administration and Development* 30, no. 1 (2010): 2–10, doi.org/10.1002/pad.559.
4   Gordon Peake, 'Understanding International Police Organisations: What the Researchers Do Not See', *Journal of International Peacekeeping* 14, no. 3–4 (2010): 425–45, doi.org/10.1163/187541110X504409; Sinclair Dinnen and Gordon Peake, 'Experimentation and Innovation in Police Reform', *Political Science* 67, no. 1 (2015): 21–37, doi.org/10.1177/0032318715580623; Eric Scheye and Gordon Peake, 'To Arrest Insecurity: Time for a Revised Security Sector Reform Agenda', *Conflict, Security & Development* 5, no. 3 (2005): 295–327, doi.org/10.1080/14678800500344564.

Moreover, as in any form of relationship, success depends upon the willingness and levels of interest of the people involved, and their incentives. If people are not interested, or simply regard showing up to work as a means of acquiring a salary – a most understandable goal in a place with such high levels of unemployment – there really is not much one can do. Yet, in my experiences in international development, writing about issues of interest and levels of engagement was off-limits. That was a topic for after-work drinks, or ventilation on messaging platforms, but not for the official record. Another taboo issue was the extent to which the adviser was expected to advise on an issue at a remove from the issue itself, or even do the job themselves, a head-in-the-sand approach given that people from all over the world travel to fill positions that cannot be filled from within the place itself. It was strictly forbidden to talk about the political setting in which such work was taking place and whether such 'reforms' were desired in the first place.

'How many people work in the Bougainville government?' I asked George. The population of the place was reckoned to be 200–300,000. 'Not counting the health employees, about 500,' was the answer. *That was a very small number to do all the tasks expected of them,* I remember thinking. It was time to call it a day, and I went out the door with George to our shared accommodation, located on Sohano, a little island between Buka and Bougainville islands and only a two-minute ride away by motorised banana boat. My new home could not have been any more removed from the palatial old Dutch colonial house in Harare with our retinue of domestic staff and security guards manning the gates – although this little place also had a storied history. Sohano had been the home of German and Australian administrators, whose houses, I was told, had been located near where my home was now. Until 10 years earlier, my room had been part of a small hotel. The writer Michael Moran writes evocatively of his stay here in the early 2000s, with war photographs affixed to the walls and a vase of knitted flowers on the serving table.[5] There was little of this faded glory now. When I was there it carried the air of a partitioned flophouse. There was a table, a TV with a satellite box showing BBC news and 30 Indonesian cable channels, a rattan chair and a squeaky bed. I was taking over the room of my predecessor, and her predecessor before that. I felt like the latest in a long conveyor belt of personnel.

---

5   Michael Moran, *Beyond the Coral Sea: Travels in the Old Empires of the South-west Pacific* (London: Harper Collins, 2004).

3

Make-work and workshops

I found myself in 'make-work' mode after a week or so in Buka. The feeling reminded me of how I had felt occasionally in Dili when there was nothing to do, in a combination of enervation, ennui and Catholic guilt at being monetarily compensated for not doing very much. But Dili had been a big enough place that if one didn't have something to do immediately, there were plenty of ways to pass the time. In Buka, with a population about one-hundredth the size, there was not. My job putatively gave me a roving brief, but it was difficult to locate people to work with. The government was made up of 14 ministries with grandiloquent titles – 'Personnel Management and Administrative Services'; 'Lands, Physical Planning, Environment and Conservation'; 'Police, Corrective Services and Justice' – but there were often fewer people inside the offices than there were words in the title of the department. The government was stone-broke: grants received from PNG covered salaries but not much else. (In the years I worked in Bougainville, the government itself generated less than 5 million kina [about A$2 million] per annum of its own revenue.)[1] The sliding gate to the entrance of the main government office block was off its runners, and driving in and out of the small government complex necessitated navigating a cavernous pothole. In the offices of the Department of Primary Industries – responsible for, among other things, the forestry industry – there was a gaping hole in the wooden floorboards of the second-floor conference room.

---

1 Satish Chand, *Financing for Fiscal Autonomy: Fiscal Self-Reliance in Bougainville*, PNG National Research Institute Research Report 3 (2018): 11, www.abg.gov.pg/uploads/documents/Financing_for_fiscal_autonomy-_Fiscal_Self-reliance_in_Bougainville_.pdf.

The creation of this government was one of the features of the Peace Agreement that ended the Crisis of 1988–97, the longest-running and most deadly conflict in the Pacific since the Second World War.[2] The parties agreed[3] that Bougainville would be granted a special political status – autonomy – in the interim, leading to a constitutionally guaranteed referendum on Bougainville's future political status. The referendum was to happen no less than 10 and no more than 15 years after the establishment of the autonomous government on Bougainville, which meant it had to happen before the middle of 2020. The result of the referendum would be non-binding in nature, final decision-making authority resting with the PNG parliament.

Hundreds of copies of the Peace Agreement sat around the government offices, some still reposing in the cardboard boxes they had been shipped in. Other boxes contained the amendments to the Constitution of PNG and an *Organic Law on Peace-building in Bougainville – Autonomous Bougainville Government and Bougainville Referendum* (2002) that gave effect to the agreement, as well as a separate constitution for the region. The documents are written in precise, necessarily detailed legal English. Edward Wolfers, an academic and adviser to the PNG government during the peace negotiations, tallied the documents he believed were required to be understood to gain full familiarity with the autonomy arrangements; when I printed them all, they came to nearly 400 double-sided pages.[4] There was limited understanding of this complex system: the autonomy arrangements reminded me of having an old computer, not understanding the operating system, and never getting around to reading the manual. Moreover, because of the passage of time, many of the political leaders from Bougainville and PNG[5] who crafted the Peace Agreement had since left the stage.

While there was a heavy focus on 'which' new institutions were to be created, there seemed to have been less of a focus on 'who' and 'how', namely, the people and skills required to animate these institutions.

---

2   Anthony J. Regan, *Light Intervention: Lessons from Bougainville* (Washington, DC: US Institute of Peace Press, 2010).

3   Braithwaite et al., *Reconciliation and Architectures*, 56–58.

4   Edward P. Wolfers, 'Bougainville Autonomy – Implementation for Governance and Decentralisation', *Contemporary PNG Studies: DWU Research Journal* 6 (May, 2007): 92–101.

5   Parliamentary Bipartisan Committee on Bougainville Affairs, 'Implementing the Bougainville Peace Agreement: Pertinent Issues and Challenges' (unpublished document, April 2017, PDF file), 15.

Giving a title and nameplate to a government department is easy; finding the people who can discharge the functions expected of it is not. People can't just be magicked up with the skills to manage human resources, design and direct infrastructure projects, manage financial grants and churn out papers. As Sue Ingram writes in her doctoral thesis: 'The public service was hollowed out by the conflict: senior public servants and many well-educated Bougainvilleans fled and remade their lives elsewhere, leaving a lasting skills deficit.'[6]

The everyday effect of this sometimes felt like inertia. By the time I gained access to my office, I felt as if whatever energy had been metabolised into my job description was like last year's trade wind, long since passed.

Ingram writes that 'much of the governance machinery … remains to be built, and most of the available functions and powers are yet to be exercised'.[7] In such a condition, how could this administration be supported?

The question placed the program I was working on, and others like it, in a distinct bind and indicated the limited extent to which money alone – the only currency at our disposal – could address the matters at hand. Officially, I was working as part of a funded 'partnership' between the governments of Australia, New Zealand, PNG and Bougainville. Australia put in most of the money and New Zealand a little, the other two governments contributing via a process of voodoo accounting that I never fully understood. We were allocated an annual budget, and our job was to help the governments develop projects geared towards improving their effectiveness. Easy to say, very difficult to do. For some in the Bougainville government, at least, our project was correlated with elaborating fulsome requests to travel to Port Moresby for the purpose of holding meetings. Paying for costs of meetings is easy. It is much harder to find the currency that can nudge development of the critical thinking skills required to grapple with the mundane complexities of government. Such support is difficult, time-consuming and unglamorous, and no-one has yet worked out what effectiveness looks like. Having funds around also created a 'honey-pot' effect, advertising that donor aid was there to be accessed and benefited from. This was a long-standing practice.

---

6   Sue Ingram, 'Post-Conflict Political Settlements and the Quest for Stability: The Cases of Timor-Leste and Bougainville' (PhD dissertation, The Australian National University, 2016), 246.
7   Ingram, 'Post-Conflict Political Settlements', 215.

During the peace process, AusAID, Australia's development agency (now part of the Department of Foreign Affairs and Trade, DFAT), had become a Tok Pisin expression for 'easy money'.

Another problem, one not peculiar to Bougainville, was how programs such as the one I was working on could predict what would occur and when. Aid is a managerialist business; problems are pre-identified, outcomes are pre-specified, the time frames in which they are to be accomplished rigidly set, the number of days in which an activity is to take place noted with actuarial precision, with activities to be mapped out in month-by-month boxes. Unacknowledged was the fact that the most difficult thing to predict is the future. Papua New Guinea confounded those trying to plot a rational course or elaborate a grand strategy, which made it all the more bewildering that everyone seemed so obsessed with developing long-range plans. Even though Papua New Guineans referred to their country in a fatalistic, gallows-humour way as 'the Land of the Unexpected' – it was even their tourism campaign's catchphrase – this nod to uncertainty failed to permeate aid programming. Some aid plans would be worthy of the Supreme Soviet; when I checked 'Properties' for the metadata settings on one of our documents, the original author was revealed to be a program in Communist Vietnam.

I spent a few days in my new office delving deeper into the work of my predecessors. I came across a cutting from a New Zealand newspaper about a volunteer from the country's aid program, a middle-aged woman named Donna, who had been helping to develop a lands policy and a land law for the region. The story was written in the boosterish style of the small-town feature writer but provided firm evidence that a lot of work had been undertaken. As part of her volunteering, Donna assisted in organising a 'lands summit' a few years prior to my arrival. A weighty report from the summit sat in the files, complete with pictures, charts and details of further steps. This was worthwhile and important work: land use had been among the issues driving the Crisis,[8] and the Bougainville constitution[9] specified that one of the jobs of the government was to develop a new lands policy and land law. Going by the reports, a great

---

8   Regan, *Light Intervention*, 13; Ogan, 'Bougainville Conflict', 5.
9   'The Constitution of the Autonomous Region of Bougainville 2004', paclii.org/pg/constitution-bougainville-2004.html.

deal of time and effort had clearly been invested, so I went to the relevant department to see how much of it had seeded, and if there was anything I could help with.

The office was behind a trade store and consisted of three partitioned rooms. In one of the rooms I found the department's secretary in his office; in familiar form, the office was crammed full of old filing boxes and mouldered newspapers, as well as computerised maps of Bougainville showing the two main islands, the atolls and the islets that made up the region. The maps were the work of a new volunteer, who was seated in one of the other rooms and working on what I presumed was a new set of maps.

The secretary's name was William. He was in his mid-sixties, had tightly cropped hair and wore a short-sleeved shirt with a small penguin insignia. He had an easy explanation for why, four years on from the summit, there had been no progress. 'It's simple,' he said. 'We have no money. If there was funding, we could do lots of things. Donor partners need to be supporting us.' 'Donor partners' was one of the phrases used frequently, and, speaking to William, I felt as if all the work of volunteer Donna had vanished. I was to hear a variant of this remark repeatedly from several people during my time in Bougainville, this rusted-on sense that money was needed to progress all activities. Some bureaucrats, but by no means all, ascribed a very specific meaning to 'money'. It did not connote paying for a computer system, software licensing or training courses in relevant subject matters. Money was correlated with having meetings, with personal benefit accruing: paid-for travel to meetings, and catering allowances.

Fearing more idle days ahead, I suggested that we crack into the funds I had at hand. 'We'll pay for food, and let's have a half-day meeting to figure out how to progress this lands policy,' I said, hoping that offering lunch might generate some energy. William was amenable to the idea, if not exactly aflame about it. He asked me if there was any funding for a trip to Port Moresby or a study trip to Vanuatu instead – I'd mentioned that this neighbouring Pacific country had recently revised its own land law.[10] Despite William's preference for something more ambitious, a meeting

---

10 Siobhan McDonnell, 'Better Protection for Custom Owners: Key Changes in Vanuatu's New Land Legislation', *Outrigger: Blog of the Pacific Institute*, 4 March 2021, pacificinstitute.anu.edu. au/outrigger/2014/03/04/better-protection-for-custom-owners-key-changes-in-vanuatus-new-land-legislation/.

was duly arranged in Buka for a few days' hence, to be held in another thinly peopled office in the Department of Education, next door to the Australian-built court complex.

I was a bit worried to begin with because no-one was there at the start time, but people began trickling in after about half an hour, an early indication of the elasticity of time here. (Only Catholic masses ever seemed to start on time.) Along, too, came the minister, a softly spoken man called John Tabinaman, who told me that this day, St Patrick's Day, was an auspicious day to begin this event, given my provenance, and that he'd been taught by Irish missionaries. They'd taught him about the wonders of independence, he said. 'They'd always spit when the national anthem was played and refused to say "God Save the Queen",' he said, smiling.

We began with a prayer; then the minister spoke. He acknowledged that progress on the land law had been slender over the last few years, but that he hoped this meeting would rejuvenate matters. He then set everyone the task of completing the whole process of developing a land law by the middle of the year. His time frame flummoxed me. Nothing had happened for years, and suddenly an arbitrary and fantastical deadline was plucked from the sky.

I had offered to facilitate the meeting as part of a desperate attempt to try to be useful and had brought along a flipchart, some marker pens and a can-do attitude. I told the assembled who I was, how I was in no way an expert on Bougainville lands policy, and that my role was simply to ask a few directive questions and be a scribe for their thoughts. To help them focus, I had printed off copies of the report from yesteryear the previous day and dropped them off at the office.

I thought I'd start with a gentle warm-up question: 'What is a policy, and why is it important?'

Silence; no response from anyone. No-one seemed to have brought the report to even leaf through, which was evidence for my supposition that nobody read this stuff. However, such an epiphany was not helpful for the purpose of pushing along conversation. William folded his arms, a few staff members started writing on the notebooks, and one began playing on his phone. The silence surprised me – for the month I'd been here thus far, and on the occasions when I could locate relevant people in their offices – the provision of new 'policies' and 'laws' had been constantly touted as the solution to all problems.

The air conditioner had clapped out by now, and I could feel the trickles of sweat on my skin becoming a stream, amplifying the ticking of the clock, the sound of which was cacophonous in this silent room. I felt like a comedian who didn't realise how uninspiring his prepared material was until he bounded up on stage.

I tried a different approach, recalling something I'd read – namely, that people work more effectively when they are organised around solving specific, definable problems rather than creating abstract treatises. 'Let's try to list all the problems involving land in Bougainville,' I suggested. This approach inspired responsiveness. *Thank Christ!* 'No rules around building in Buka Town,' said William, referring to the laissez-faire approach to construction that seemed to prevail. I wrote this down on the chart. 'No clear rules for customary land,' said Zoe, a young woman with doe eyes and a can-do sense of enthusiasm. More than 97 per cent of the land in Bougainville (and all parts of PNG) was customary,[11] held and dealt with according to customary rules, as defined by the local community.[12] 'No means to register land ownership,' said Rooney, a recent graduate. 'No computers,' said another, a valid point. We talked about the platforms and systems that would be needed to solve these problems. The group was fired up. Ideas flowed. Time moved quickly, and we had a short lunch before continuing into the afternoon, past even the peculiarly precise mandated public service finishing time of 4:06 pm, the time it had been under the Australian colonial administration.

By the end of the session we'd chunked down into three pages the problems bound up with land issues in Bougainville, a long list of what were called 'burning issues'. I suggested that the fabled process of policymaking was nothing magical but merely a step-by-step iteration of a response to each of these issues. It didn't have to be a long or windy document, just an itemised listing of how one could respond to each identified problem: it could involve using an existing law better (PNG law prevailed until Bougainville developed its own) or it could be logistical, such as improving office organisation. The next day, we mapped out a series of necessarily boring next steps: who was going to do research on what; who was going to attain a better understanding of what the land law said on this or that matter. It was stimulating and motivating for us all and seemed to be

11   Regan, *Light Intervention*, 11.
12   Douglas Oliver, *Black Islanders: A Personal Perspective of Bougainville 1937–91* (South Yarra: Hyland House, 1991), 106.

the start of something worthwhile. We held a subsequent meeting the following week in which we honed plans. The meeting again ran past time and included 25 boxes of chicken and chips ordered from the Hot Rooster shop to give everyone the energy to continue.

At the beginning, I felt I was witnessing the trajectory I'd read about time and time again: initial enthusiasm, bursts of effort and then … utter stillness, until the idea itself descended into its own dusty folder. About six months later, a letter came in on government letterhead requesting funding for a trip to Vanuatu to study the land law there, and a month after that, a proposal for a new building.

Then, in the months and the years ahead – just as I was starting to feel forlorn, careworn and cynical – the ideas we talked about during those days reared up unexpectedly and unbidden, like one of the dolphins cavorting in the Buka Passage. In the months and the years to come, we had more sessions to help progress the lands policy, to break down the lunchtime 'burning issues' into practical solutions. A new secretary called Raphael came in to replace William, who had reached his retirement age. Other advisers took up the baton: a former Papua New Guinean magistrate and an Australian who replaced the lawyer with the Johnny Cash couture. In 2021, long after I left, long after it was promised in the work-plan, the lands policy was finalised and a law was being drafted. Things happened, but not according to a timetable I could control, and almost always when it was unexpected.

This pattern of rise and fall, and sometimes rise again, recurred frequently throughout my years in Bougainville, such as when I tried to set up a board to regulate the price of commodities, or strove to improve the efforts of the government to collect the one tax it was responsible for. The pattern characterised my work on fisheries management and my attempts to create a licensing scheme. There would be a pledge to work 'around the clock on an issue', a flurry of meetings, and a dawning awareness of the long-lasting and difficult tasks bound up in progressing even a sliver of the task. Then the issue would recede from view, like a cargo ship silently sailing over the horizon, to return someday – maybe. On some days it felt like I was living inside what Harvard scholars called a capability trap, in which 'they [in this case, government employees] cannot perform the tasks asked of them, and doing the same thing day after day is not improving the situation'.[13] I would also recognise that in this scenario there are elements of what Max Everest-Phillips calls '*bureaupathology*, or the condition of anxiety and insecurity due to alienation, limited promotion prospects, less-than-adequate pay and conditions of work, pessimism, sense of powerlessness'.[14] The public servants were to be saluted for staying the course.

But there were other days on which it seemed that the people within this administration were capable of accomplishing the most unexpected things.

As I was writing this book I came across an article by Alex Golub about the bureaucracy of Papua New Guinea's police force that encapsulated what I was experiencing:

> Much of what counts as … 'functioning institutions' in Melanesia owe their success less to bureaucratic regularity than to the hard work of local actors […] Local actors do not fail the State, the State fails them – and it is only due to their hard work that they are able to keep it ticking over.[15]

I went on to write an article with a colleague from The Australian National University about these hard-working and dogged bureaucrats who leverage their histories, connections and affiliations to get things done, just as these bureaucrats did when trying to tackle land issues in Bougainville, which felt at times like the stickiest of bureaupathology problems.[16] We are too silent on the importance of these individual actors. Let's name them and give them at least the acclaim that can be acquired in a book. There is Zoe, there is Rooney, and there are others like them, trying their hardest in exceptionally difficult circumstances.

13   Lant Pritchett, Michael Woolcock and Matt Andrews, 'Capability Traps? The Mechanisms of Persistent Implementation Failure' (Working Paper 234, Center for Global Development, Washington, DC, 2010): 2, cgdev.org/publication/capability-traps-mechanisms-persistent-implementation-failure-working-paper-234.
14   Max Everest-Phillips, *Small, So Simple? Complexity in Small Island Developing States*, (Singapore: UNDP Global Centre for Public Service Excellence, 2014), docslib.org/doc/7961786/small-so-simple-complexity-in-small-island-developing-states-author-max-everest-phillips.
15   Alex Golub, 'Introduction: The Politics of Order in Contemporary Papua New Guinea', *Anthropological Forum* 28, no. 4 (2018): 331–41, doi.org/10.1080/00664677.2018.1545108.
16   Gordon Peake and Miranda Forsyth, 'Street-level Bureaucrats in a Relational State: The Case of Bougainville', *Public Administration and Development* 1, no. 42 (2021): 12–21, doi.org/10.1002/pad.1911.

4

Bookanville

Just as one should never judge a book by its cover, one should never judge a library by its external appearance. I grew up near a small town in Northern Ireland called Downpatrick, whose library was never going to make any exquisite decor lists. Pebble-dashed in varieties of dirty brown, the building's severe exterior gave little clue to the joys found within. I can trace a life's love of reading to that library, graduating from picture books to Enid Blyton, to a brilliant but now little-remembered series for aspiring young detectives called *Alfred Hitchcock and the Three Investigators*, to the English thriller writer Hammond Innes, to Stephen King, to Paul Theroux, and then on to books that explained Northern Ireland's tangled history while indicating there was a world to be explored beyond my little town. I can't remember a lot about the South Seas in the collection, but do recall vividly an illustrated photo book detailing Thor Heyerdahl's voyage across the Pacific in the *Kon-Tiki*.

Thoughts about the building and its contents came to mind when I first saw Buka's Unity Library, the exterior of which was even more unprepossessing. The library was located behind a rusted chain-link fence on the bottom floor of a two-storey house built on the grounds of a decommissioned fuel station. Between the barrier and the house were two sets of concrete steps that led to nothing more than thin air, some sort of prescient metaphor. The house overlooked the waters of the passage, the airport that welcomed the daily flight from Port Moresby, and Buka Town's tiny sprawl.

The library was the initiative of an Australian woman called Lesley Palmer, who was a more productive and good-natured trailing spouse than I had been. Pat, her husband, was managing a program supporting the region's courts and police at the same time as I was in Bougainville. Each Friday night he hosted the '4:06 club drinks' –'4:06' being a reference to the 4:06 pm knock-off time – at which various advisers working with the government would seek solace and solidarity in beer. Spurred by visits to nearby schools, and finding that often the only book to be found was the one painted on the school crest, Lesley converted the space below their living quarters into a library. She assembled thousands of books provided by supporters from Australia, affixed educational posters to the walls and created a little enclave of the imagination. Most of the library's clientele were school-aged children. They'd line up like acolytes of the Pied Piper outside the door to gain entrance. Among the staff was Tania, an outrageously talented photographer, and Steph, a woman who wanted to be a writer but was paralysed by thinking that writing was something others did, not she. 'Every writer in the world has this fear, this insecurity,' I told her. This wasn't idle flim-flam on my part; I knew exactly how she felt.

I'd finished the novels I'd bought in the airport in Johannesburg on the way over and was happy to find a library here. I found solace in the books I borrowed from Unity every bit as much as I had in those of my childhood. Although happy I had a job, I fought bouts of loneliness that felt especially acute on the many days when there was nothing to do. I missed Suzanne and I missed my boys. I didn't want to succumb to drink, had no interest in indulging in an unhappy affair, as some had done before me, and found comfort, as I always have, in the pages of books.

Most of the books I sought out were about the history of Bougainville.[1] I supplemented these with material found in online libraries and, later, visits to the National Library of Australia, and archives in both Canberra and Oxford. I read about Louis de Bougainville,[2] the French

1   Douglas Oliver, *Bougainville: A Personal History* (Carlton, Vic: Melbourne University Press, 1973); Oliver, *Black Islanders*; Donald Denoon, *Getting Under the Skin: The Bougainville Copper Agreement and the Creation of the Panguna Mine* (Carlton, Vic: Melbourne University Press, 2000); Anthony J. Regan and Helga M. Griffin, eds, *Bougainville before the Conflict* (Canberra: ANU Press, 2015), doi.org/10.22459/BBC.08.2015; Josephine Tankunani Sirivi and Marilyn Taleo Havini, *As Mothers of the Land: The Birth of the Bougainville Women for Peace and Freedom* (Canberra: Pandanus Books and the Research School of Pacific and Asian Studies, The Australian National University, 2004).
2   Victor Suthren, *The Sea Has No End: The Life of Louis-Antoine de Bougainville* (Toronto: Dundurn, 2004).

navigator who sailed up the passage in 1768, naming everything around him, blithely unaware of indigenous names, in classic colonial fashion. He named the larger island after himself and the smaller one 'Buka' after the sound he reported was made by the people when they rowed out to his boat. 'Buka' means 'who' in one of the local languages, a not unreasonable question to ask when spotting an unfamiliar vessel with billowing sails.

The French captain did not return after naming the islands, which were left in relatively splendid isolation from the outside world until Richard Parkinson, a Danish naturalist and adventurer, arrived more than a century later to collect artefacts and natural history specimens. In his book *Thirty Years in the South Seas*, Parkinson wrote that he was the first white person to cross the passage between the two islands.[3] While this may have been the case, we know that whalers and traders also called in on Bougainville from the early 1800s. In the mid- to late 1800s, blackbirders came, too, slavers who kidnapped islanders or tricked them onto their ships, then ferried them to Australia to work on plantations.

The Germans assumed formal charge in 1884 and divvied up territory with the British in typical colonial fashion by signing a document far away from the place itself. That document was an early forerunner to the formal documents and memorandums of understanding (MoUs) with which the present-day government seems obsessed.

In reality, the Kaiser's 'rule' consisted of little more than the occasional visit to the coast by white-suited and topee-topped Germans on their coal-fired steamers. The Germans[4] primarily regarded Bougainville as a source of good, strong and reliable labour. 'Buka boys' were to be found throughout the German and British Pacific as police officers, house servants and boatmen. Hugh Romilly, an administrator in British New Guinea, wrote in 1886 that: 'Buka men … are the finest specimens of manhood in the South Seas […] [W]herever he goes, a Buka man will always be a leader.'[5] I photographed the quote and sent it to a few Bougainvillean friends via WhatsApp, former combatants now eking out existences doing security

3   Richard Parkinson, *Thirty Years in the South Seas* (Sydney NSW: Sydney University Press, 2010).
4   Peter Sack, 'German Colonial Rule in the Northern Solomons', in *Bougainville before the Conflict*, ed. Anthony J. Regan and Helga M. Griffin (Canberra: ANU Press, 2015), 77–107, doi.org/10.22459/BBC.08.2015.
5   Hugh Romilly, *The Western Pacific and New Guinea* (second edition) (London: John Murray, 1887). Although Buka is many times smaller than Bougainville, 'Bukas' was the term used in the colonial era to describe people from the whole of Bougainville.

work for the government, for which they were rarely paid. I received replies immediately, all along the lines of: 'Even the white man ... knows we are stronger than anyone else. Independence *nau!*'

I also read about the islands' underacknowledged role in Second World War, about the Japanese occupation, and the American and Australian campaigns to wrest the islands back from the Japanese, which included the troop-rallying of Bob Hope, the undistinguished military career of Richard Milhous Nixon and the baseball diamonds that American troops carved out of the cleared jungle. When the Americans held movie nights in their bases, both Japanese and local Bougainvilleans would sneak up to the fence to watch the images.[6] By head count, most victims of the war were Japanese: according to historian Hank Nelson, more than 40,000 Japanese troops died in the islands. Bougainville itself, however, also suffered enormous losses. Nelson estimates that more than a quarter of the pre–Second World War population of Bougainville perished.[7]

I read about the search for gold and other precious minerals that long drew prospectors and fortune-hunters here, as elsewhere in New Guinea.[8] Speckled like gold dust within the accounts of anthropologists, planters (growers of coconuts and cocoa) and naturalists, and those of soldiers fighting on Bougainville, are the stories of frequently unsuccessful prospecting expeditions that failed to dim the strong conviction that riches lay there somewhere, if only the right place could be located.

In the early 1960s, around a decade after the first government school opened, Australian geologists discovered a massive, low-grade ore body (0.6% or less), containing mainly copper and gold, but also some silver and molybdenum, and occupying a huge area in the middle of the main island of Bougainville (often referred to as Bougainville Island), near a mountain called Panguna.[9] Locally, a key feature of the topography, a rugged outcrop called Pankiranku that was of spiritual significance to

6   Harry A. Gailey, *Bougainville 1943–1945: The Forgotten Campaign* (Kentucky: The University Press of Kentucky, 1991); Karl James, *The Hard Slog: Australians in the Bougainville Campaign, 1944–45* (Cambridge, UK: Cambridge University Press, 2012), doi.org/10.1017/CBO9781139196307.

7   Hank Nelson, 'Bougainville in World War II', in *Bougainville before the Conflict*, ed. Anthony J. Regan and Helga M. Griffin (Canberra: ANU Press, 2015), 196, doi.org/10.22459/BBC.08.2015.

8   Chris Ballard, 'The Signature of Terror: Violence, Memory and Landscape at Freeport', in *Inscribed Landscapes: Marking and Making Place*, ed. Bruno David and Meredith Wilson (Honolulu: University of Hawaii Press, 2002), 15; Denise Leith, *The Politics of Power: Freeport in Suharto's Indonesia* (Honolulu: University of Hawaii Press, 2002), 1.

9   Jackson, Graham, Moore & Partners, *Bougainville Mining Limited: A Fundamental Evaluation* (Sydney: Jackson, Graham, Moore & Partners, 1971).

the local Nasioi villagers, was destroyed when the mine site was cleared. The pit that was subsequently gouged out of the mountain was one of the largest human-made holes in the world. The engineers laid down sets of giant piping under the concrete on the road that would connect to a purpose-built port. To house the mineworkers, two towns were built: one close to the mine site, called Panguna, and one called Arawa, built on top of a copra and cocoa plantation that had previously housed a magnificent orchid collection. Into this new town came thousands, many of them of Bougainvilleans, but also people from elsewhere in PNG and a smaller number of expatriates, mostly Australians, who created a mirror image of an Australian country town in the tropics.

Among the frequently requested books in the library were those of recent vintage[10] telling the story of a 10-year conflict that began a year before the Berlin Wall fell. People here called this time 'the Crisis'. It was part ethnic in nature, pitting Bougainvilleans against the Papua New Guinean army and police,[11] while other elements of the Crisis were more akin to civil war. It was a conflict in 'which many had no proud ideas', wrote Bougainvillean academic and novelist Regis Tove Stella.[12]

The pre-eminent chronicler of this period is a man who had an office a few doors down from mine when I worked in Canberra at ANU. His name is Anthony Regan. Regan worked on Bougainville for more than 40 years. He first travelled there in 1978 to visit his sister, who was married to a Bougainvillean, and went on to do legal work for successive Bougainville governments since 1981, including service as a legal adviser during the peace negotiations. He continues to fulfil an advisory role in an informal capacity. Regan has done more than any other person to help broaden understandings of historical and contemporary Bougainville.[13] I like Anthony a lot; he was always a gracious colleague to me when we both worked in Canberra, and generous with his knowledge and expertise when we worked together in Buka.

10   Braithwaite et al., *Reconciliation and Architectures,* 161; Ronald J. May and Matthew Spriggs, eds., *The Bougainville Crisis* (Bathurst, NSW: Crawford House Publishing, 1990); Sirivi and Havini, *Mothers of the Land;* Sean Dorney, *The Sandline Affair: Politics and Mercenaries and the Bougainville Crisis* (Sydney: ABC Books for the Australian Broadcasting Corporation, 1998).

11   Regan, *Light Intervention,* 20.

12   Regis Tove Stella, *Gutsini Posa* (Suva, Mana Publications, 1999).

13   Many of Regan's contributions are cited in this text. Further readings are listed on his Google Scholar profile; see 'Anthony J. Regan', *Google Scholar,* scholar.google.com/citations?user=Ac6GQ6 UAAAAJ&hl=en.

There is no one answer as to how the Crisis began. As the copper gushed, elements of disgruntlement, jealousies and slights among the Bougainvilleans were morphing, sticking and intermingling into combustible compounds.

Five elements emerged. The first was frustration that the government of PNG, which became independent from Australia in 1975, was receiving the bulk of royalties from the mine,[14] with only a dribble going back to Bougainville's provincial government. Element two involved the dissatisfaction of landowners close to the mine with low payments for the use and destruction of their land,[15] and, particularly, with the uneven distribution of this money among different groups, suffusing the mountainscapes and valleys with jealousy.[16] The third element was the Bougainvillean mineworkers' unhappiness with the terms and conditions of their employment, especially as compared to the conditions enjoyed by expatriates and 'redskins' (Papua New Guineans from other provinces).[17] Fourthly, tensions were bubbling between Bougainvilleans and migrants in PNG who had arrived in search of income opportunities.[18] Bougainvillean salaries were the same as those of the 'redskins' (all of them far lower than those of expatriates). There was however, some resentment about Bougainvilleans not being promoted into BCL (Bougainville Copper Ltd, the mining company in question) low and middle-level management positions, which were held by redskins. Moreover, standards of housing were graded from low to high 'covenant' (as elsewhere in colonial PNG, including Port Moresby), and those employed in low-status jobs (all being 'redskin' or Bougainvillean) had access only to 'low covenant' housing.

---

14   Ogan, 'Bougainville Conflict', 5.

15   Richard Bedford and Alexander Mamak, *Compensating for Development: The Bougainville Case* (Christchurch: University of Canterbury, 1977), 7; John Connell, 'Compensation and Conflict: The Bougainville Copper Mine, Papua New Guinea', in *Mining and Indigenous Peoples in Australasia*, ed. John Connell and Richard Howitt (Melbourne: Sydney University Press, 1991), 61; Ciaran O'Faircheallaigh, *Mining and Development* (Kent: Croom Helm, 1984), 220; Paul Quodling, *Bougainville – the Mine and the People* (St Leonards: Centre for Independent Studies, 1991), 52.

16   Colin Filer, David Henton and Richard Jackson, *Landowner Compensation in Papua New Guinea's Mining and Petroleum Sectors* (Port Moresby: PNG Chamber of Mines and Petroleum, 2000); Quodling, *Mine and People*, 52.

17   Jill Nash and Eugene Ogan, 'The Red and the Black: Bougainvillean Perceptions of Other Papua New Guineans', *Pacific Studies* 13, no. 2 (1990), 1–17.

18   Benedict Y. Imbun, 'Mining Workers or "Opportunist" Tribesmen? A Tribal Workforce in a Papua New Guinea Mine', *Oceania* 71, no. 2 (2000), 129–49.

These four elements fused with a fifth factor, the underlying unhappiness among some Bougainvilleans at being part of PNG in the first place. A sense of distinctness and separateness predated the opening of the mine.[19] In 1962, local leaders told a visiting United Nations delegation that the Australians treated the Bougainvilleans like dogs, and that the administration of the islands should be turned over to the Americans, of whom there were still fond memories after the Second World War. Australian government patrol officers who visited Bougainvillean villages around that time describe in their reports the conversations they had with village chiefs, who said Bougainville should be left alone and not form part of any other country. Independence was their singing flame.

Later, in the national libraries in Port Moresby and Canberra, I found assorted copies of the *Arawa Bulletin*, the town's weekly newspaper. The *Bulletin* is filled with no end of delicious, newsy nuggets familiar to anyone growing up in a small town in the 1970s or 1980s, with their own idiosyncratic island twists: kids' puzzles about Tok Pisin terms for commonplace words, recipe tips (12 things to do with sweet potato), an anonymous column in which no end of scurrilous gossip was aired, and an over-the-top set of passive aggressive letters to the editor, signed off with pre-internet *noms de plume* such as 'Dissatisfied' or 'Waiting an Explanation'. Here's a representative example:

> The Queen's visit to Bougainville and especially Arawa was a very exciting time for everyone but I must express my disappointment at the very poor representation of the Arawa group of Brownie guides. ('Disappointed')

Excessive alcohol and its ill-effects were perennial themes. Much of the editor's postbag in May of 1979 revolved around a labyrinthine 'he-said-she-said' as to whether a bacchanalian bevy of Hash House Harriers had gatecrashed a teenage girl's birthday party or had been invited to it.

There was a lot of politics in the *Arawa Bulletin* nonetheless. Wedged between the reports from the squash league and the darts ladder in one of the April 1975 editions was a one-page advertisement labelled the 'People's Decision', stating that Bougainvilleans were insecure about joining with PNG and would prefer to go it alone. A few months later,

---

19   James Griffin, 'Movements towards Secession 1964–76', in *Bougainville before the Conflict*, ed. Anthony J. Regan and Helga M. Griffin (Canberra: ANU Press, 2015), 291–99, doi.org/10.22459/BBC.08.2015.

the provincial government did just that. Bougainville made a 'Unilateral Declaration of Independence' in 1975.[20] However, a country can only become 'independent' in the view of the world if other countries recognise it. Bougainville's declaration of independence went unnoticed. Australia, New Zealand and the rest of the world ignored it. I could find no record in newspapers (apart from the *Arawa Bulletin*) that the declaration ever took place.

Years later, these compound elements became quicksilver in the hands of Francis Ona, landowner from near the mine site and a university-educated surveyor who became a haul-truck operator at the mine because it paid better. Ona was in his early thirties. He formed a group who called themselves the Bougainville Revolutionary Army – BRA for short, the name a nod to the zeitgeist of the times. In 1988, Ona and his team used dynamite pilfered from company stores to blow up electricity pylons, as well as committing other minor instances of industrial sabotage. Their initial stated aim was to create pressure for an improved share of royalties, and better terms and conditions for themselves, but soon their cause took on a nationalist dimension, connecting back to ideas of independence and referendums.[21] Some dubbed the rebels 'rambos' after Sylvester Stallone's character in the movie *Rambo: First Blood Part II*, which was being shown in a regular loop on the island's one TV channel.[22] Macho naming conventions may have been inspired also by the weekly diet of 'rock 'em, sock 'em' movies on release at the cinemas up in Panguna. In the closest *Arawa Bulletin* I could find to the beginning of the Crisis, the films being screened were action–adventure fare, including *Kampuchea Express, Eye of the Needle, Forgotten Warrior, Arctic Heat, Bruce Lee: We Miss You* and *Nine Deaths of the Ninja*.

The response of the Papua New Guinean security forces was akin to pouring water on an electrical fire. Their actions served less to restore order than to further inflame resentment and discontent.[23] Bougainvilleans fled into Arawa from villages around the mine, some of the internally

---

20   Regan, *Light Intervention*, 15.
21   Regan, *Light Intervention*, 20.
22   George P. Cosmatos, dir., *Rambo: First Blood Part II*, (Los Angeles: Carolco Pictures, 1985).
23   Regan, *Light Intervention*, 21. See also Amnesty International, *Papua New Guinea: 'Under the Barrel of a Gun': Bougainville 1991 to 1993*, ASA 34/005/1993, 19 November 1993, amnesty.org/en/documents/asa34/005/1993/en/; Amnesty International, *Papua New Guinea: Bougainville: The Forgotten Human Rights Tragedy*, 26 February 1997, ASA 34/001/1997, amnesty.org/en/documents/asa34/001/1997/en/.

displaced taking up residence in the grounds of the country club. The club's committee was outraged, but not for the reasons one might expect. An emergency meeting was called, the upshot of which is recorded in one of the last issues of the *Arawa Bulletin*. 'Displaced villagers will not be allowed to go on the golf course and the tennis court,' the committee decreed. The committee's snootiness was rendered irrelevant soon afterwards. A week later, the expats were evacuated, and the giant mining operation shut down. Over 30 years later, it is yet to reopen.

In May 1990, Ona declared Bougainville independent, with him as its leader. Australia issued a press release denouncing the rebels, while other countries ignored this declaration as pointedly as they had Bougainville's first. The declaration of independence was published in a special edition of the *Arawa Bulletin*, along with photographs of dancing bands and scouts with flags. He typed out presidential decrees on subjects as wide as the dates of public holidays and onerous visa entry requirements. He or his emissaries wrote letters to Australia, New Zealand and the Swiss ambassador in Canberra seeking international recognition but received no reply. Sporadically, from 1992 onward, leaders travelled to Geneva and Vienna to present their case to the United Nations, and to a meeting of Commonwealth leaders in Harare, but there were few indications that any country supported this would-be breakaway nation's aspirations.

* * *

Winkling out the story of what happened as the Crisis unfolded is challenging. This was not a conflict with set-piece battles, battlelines or clear sides. 'It has seemingly deteriorated into total confusion, so that not even the people of Bougainville can tell you what the situation is,' wrote an Australian Marist priest in a letter to his family.[24] In the months and years that followed, hotels and clubs were looted and burned, and shops ransacked; mining company cars were stolen, driven drunkenly around until they crashed and were stripped for scrap metal. The security forces burned houses and abused people at checkpoints; they heartlessly dangled some unfortunate people from helicopters, then flung them into the sea.[25] This was not even a conflict with two clear sides. As Anthony Regan

---

24 Kevin Kerley, *Kevin Kerley's Papers on the Bougainville Conflict and Peace Process* (The Australian National University Archives, Series 600), archivescollection.anu.edu.au/index.php/kevin-kerleys-papers-on-bougainville-conflict-and-peace-process.

25 Guy Wilson-Roberts, 'The Bougainville Conflict: An Historical Overview', in *Peace on Bougainville: Truce Monitoring Group*, ed. Rebecca Adams (Wellington: Victoria University Press, 2001), 26.

writes: 'The bitter internal conflict between Bougainvilleans undoubtedly caused more death, injury, trauma and destruction than the conflict between the PNG forces and Bougainvilleans.'[26]

Ona and his self-styled government continued to make pronouncements, but over the years he receded from view, the stage ceded to politicians whose focus seemed to be on setting up grandly titled new structures and arguing about who should occupy them. Ceasefire agreements came and went, each lauded as 'historic' despite rarely lasting long enough to justify the term. Seen to be failures at the time, they would, ultimately, lead to the structuring of an agreement that would last.[27]

In an archive at ANU in Canberra, I found the personal collection of Father Kevin Kerley, a Catholic priest who was one of the few expatriates to stay in the region during the Crisis. His archive was a glorious jumble. He had kept each and every newspaper story of those years from the *Post Courier* and clippings from the occasions when the Crisis was written up in the Australian press, along with details of every mass he had said, the numbers of confessions he had heard and baptisms he had conferred, not to mention varied ephemera such as ID cards, permission slips to buy altar wine, old Catholic mission magazines and a large collection of soft-plastic biscuit wrappers. Most of the stories were from the *Post Courier* and written in its reliably breezy style. They told of 'militants and cops trading fire'; peace initiatives lauded always as 'historic'; politicians complaining, urging, vowing and slamming; new committees set up and then forgotten; questionable uses of funds; and politicians squabbling over positions on 'authorities' that had very little authority.

And then, a twist. In an effort to end the war, which by then was close to its tenth year, the government of PNG paid millions to Sandline, a firm of British 'security consultants', to win the war for them.[28] Their efforts ended in farce. The 'consultants' were arrested by the Papua New Guinean army they had gone there to work with and slung into gaol. The prime

---

26   Anthony J. Regan, '*Mister Pip* by Lloyd Jones', review of *Mister Pip*, by Lloyd Jones, *The Journal of Pacific History* 43, no. 3 (2008): 399–401.

27   Anthony J. Regan, 'The Bougainville Political Settlement and the Prospects for Sustainable Peace', *Pacific Economic Bulletin* 17, no. 1 (2002): 116, openresearch-repository.anu.edu.au/bitstream/1885/94222/2/171_Bougainville.pdf.

28   Mary-Louise O'Callaghan, *Enemies within: Papua New Guinea, Australia, and the Sandline Crisis: The Inside Story* (Sydney: Doubleday, 1999); Anthony J. Regan and Sinclair Dinnen, 'The Sandline Affair: A Chronology of Significant Events', in *Challenging the State: The Sandline Affair in Papua New Guinea*, ed. Sinclair Dinnen, Ron May and Anthony J. Regan (Canberra: The Australian National University, 1997), 12, openresearch-repository.anu.edu.au/bitstream/1885/132682/1/PPP_30.pdf.

minister of the time, Sir Julius Chan, stood aside. A ceasefire – the tenth – was agreed to in 1998, and this one finally stuck.[29] After four years of negotiations, the Peace Agreement was signed in 2001.[30]

This war's grim literature is poignant. In Lloyd Jones's novel *Mister Pip* – shortlisted for the Man Booker Prize in 2007 – the sole remaining expatriate in Bougainville after the fighting begins uses the only book remaining on the island, Charles Dickens's *Great Expectations,* as the source material for teaching a class of orphans in a bush school outside Arawa.[31] While not to be regarded as akin to the historical record, it's a book marinated in the most stirring and poignant magical realism and made into an equally compelling film, starring Hugh Laurie and filmed, in part, on Bougainville.[32] (After the book was published, Jones set up a library in Arawa, hoping to contribute to a legacy of literature.)

Some of the most affecting writing comes from Bougainvilleans themselves. Journalist Veronica Hatutasi's *Behind the Blockade* chronicles the buckling collapse of middle-class life on the island.[33] In one chapter, she's sipping gin and tonic in an Arawa hotel, in the next, drying her children's tears when there is no Christmas. 'Santa Claus will not come because no planes are coming to our island now,' she recalls telling her children. Before the Crisis, Father Christmas used to arrive in the mining company's chopper to dispense gifts.[34] Now, helicopters were full of trigger-happy soldiers, not something to encourage children to notice. There's little need to go much farther than the title of one of Leonard Fong Roka's self-published books to get the gist: *Brokenville*.[35] His rough-hewn but grimly compelling stories feel like an almost unending descent into petty violence and village jealousies.

In the telling of the late Regis Tove Stella, an academic and writer from Bougainville, it was a conflict with little or no moral soul. Stella's novel *Gutsini Posa (Rough Seas)* lets all the protagonists have it.[36] The rebels, he

29 Regan, 'Bougainville Political Settlement', 115.
30 Anthony J. Regan, 'The Bougainville Peace Agreement, 2001–2002: Towards Order and Stability for Bougainville?', in *Arc of Instability? Melanesia in the Early 2000s*, ed. Ronald J. May (Canberra and New Zealand: The Australian National University and University of Canterbury, 2003), 9–26.
31 Lloyd Jones, *Mr Pip* (Melbourne: Text Publishing, 2006).
32 Andrew Adamson, dir., *Mr Pip* (Los Angeles, CA: Olympus Pictures), 2012.
33 Veronica Hatutasi, *Behind the Blockade* (Boroko: Word Publishing Company, 2015).
34 Hatutasi, *Behind the Blockade*, 69.
35 Leonard Fong Roka, *Brokenville* (Hervey Bay, Qld: Pukpuk Publications, 2014).
36 Stella, *Gutsini Posa*.

writes, were 'initially inebriated by nationalism' and 'lacked discipline, with people doing stupid things, shooting each other for trivial reasons, stealing from villagers, committing suicide, raping women'.[37] Penagi, the book's central character and anti-hero, joins the rebels at the end of the book. He intervenes when he sees a fellow fighter pinning down and raping a 15-year-old girl. The commander is furious. He tears into Penagi for freeing the girl. To the rapist he says not a word of reprimand.

Stella depicts government forces as equally drunken, volatile and irresponsible, siring children and quickly abandoning the mothers, responsible for midnight knocks from which people never return. He renders the politics in Port Moresby as even worse. High-minded army officers talk principles and the importance of obeying rules, but forge letters to secure Penagi's release from prison. Near the beginning of the book, a character in the novel describes Bougainville as a land of 'terrified hearts and shattered dreams', and by the end, PNG is depicted as a place of 'false hopes and broken dreams'.[38]

No-one knows for sure how many died, either directly in the conflict, or from preventable diseases and starvation. The estimated number of Bougainvilleans who perished ranges from 3,000 to 20,000.[39]

Although the Crisis ended with the Peace Agreement in 2001 and the new government was formed in 2005, scar tissue from the conflict – rivalries, old and complicated divisions, grudges and jealousies – endured. Divisions between regions about the allocation of resources have carried on.[40] The statistics on domestic violence are jarring: 80 per cent of Bougainvillean men have committed intimate partner violence.[41] A study sponsored by the United Nations revealed that just over one in four people had post-traumatic stress disorder (PTSD):

37   Stella, *Gutsini Posa*, 129.
38   Stella, *Gutsini Posa*, 8, 146.
39   Anthony J. Regan, *The Bougainville Referendum Arrangements: Origins, Shaping and Implementation. Part One: Origins and Shaping.* Department of Pacific Affairs Discussion Paper 4 (2018): 6.
40   John Connell, 'Holding on to Modernity? Siwai, Bougainville, Papua New Guinea', in *Environment, Development and Change in Rural Asia-Pacific: Between Local and Global*, ed. John Connell and Eric Waddell (London: Routledge, 2006), 127–46.
41   Emma Fulu et al., 'Prevalence of and Factors Associated with Male Perpetration of Intimate Partner Violence: Findings from the UN Multi-Country Cross-Sectional Study on Men and Violence in Asia and the Pacific', *Lancet Global Health* 1, no. 4 (2013), 187–207, doi.org/10.1016/S2214-109X(13)70074-3.

Many women said they were raped the first time they had sex …
One in three of the women who first had sex under 16 years had
been forced or raped.[42]

The study came with the obligatory ministerial foreword, an obsession
in all of PNG. The minister or, probably more accurately, the United
Nations (UN) staffer who would have drafted the remarks on his
behalf, wrote:

> This study will help us design and target more effective programs
> for the health and safety of the people of Bougainville, and we
> hope it will be used by all of our development partners in this
> shared goal.[43]

I was never able to find out whether such programs were developed.

---

42 Rachel Jewkes, Emma Fulu and Yandisa Sikweyiya, *Family, Health and Safety Study: Autonomous
Region of Bougainville, Papua New Guinea: Summary Report* (UNDP and Autonomous Bougainville
Government, 2013), www.partners4prevention.org/sites/default/files/resources/p4p-bougainville-
report.pdf.
43 Jewkes, Fulu and Sikweyiya, *Family, Health and Safety Study*.

5

Have licence, lack engine

'Let me explain the central problem of my job using the metaphor of a driving licence,' I said, as an opening to thoughts more complex. Simon and I were sitting in the Hot Rooster fried chicken shop in Buka, adjacent to another Chinese-run enterprise, Boots Camp Trading. The logo of the plump and happy-looking chicken with his or her thumbs up always reminded me of Los Pollos Hermanos, the chicken restaurant that was a front for Gustavo Fring's drug importation business in the TV series *Breaking Bad*. It was Friday lunchtime, and trade was brisk, Bougainvilleans at the kitchen broilers taking out fried chicken and chips and shovelling them into yellow and green boxes, while the young Chinese proprietor in a webbed singlet straight out of an 80s Pet Shop Boys video cross-checked each cash transaction being performed by the unhappy-looking counter staff. Unusually, he wasn't sitting on a high chair. In other stores in Buka Town, the Chinese sat on high chairs so they could watch over the tills like a tennis umpire at the net.

Observing the workaday process as we waited, I couldn't help but think how Chinese migrants were pioneering types. For all the fevered 'yellow peril' talk that occasionally bubbled up in Australian media,[1] I often thought Chinese traders in outposts like Buka were more in the business of trying to scratch out a living than of quarrying away with malign intent. Unlike me, they didn't have the prospect of a flight out every now and then. They were of hardier stock. 'That's the problem with you

1   Gareth Harvey, '60 Minutes: China's "Soft Invasion" of the South Pacific Pathway to Greater Influence', *9 News*, 17 November 2019, 9news.com.au/national/60-minutes-china-soft-invasion-of-south-pacific/71cddbe3-9afa-4b81-bd68-05f0d944c622.

white men,' a Papua New Guinean bureaucrat who headed a government department told me once. 'You're not prepared to do the hard work. You guys want toilet paper; the Chinese will happily wipe their arse with a leaf.'

We paid for our chicken and received chewing gum as change. There were rarely any coins or notes of small denomination in this or any other establishment; little orange packets of PK chewing gum were given in lieu, which I preferred anyway because they were useful in helping dispel the salty-mouth hangover that I knew would follow this fowl repast.

Simon was the head of the branch of the Australian High Commission in Port Moresby responsible for Bougainville. He didn't look like he regularly frequented fried chicken joints; he was lean and spry, and had recently returned from hiking the Kokoda Track. I liked Simon; he appreciated more than many of his colleagues that all these programs being undertaken were not the be-all and end-all of success in this country. In fact, they were rather insignificant. The total Australian aid program to PNG was around A$500 million per annum,[2] which seems a lot until one remembers that at the time, this amount was also the annual budget for an average medium-sized Australian hospital and just a small fraction of the total national budget of PNG. He was a man one could level with. At the same time, I was aware that wailing a litany of X-rated despair before we finished our first indeterminate part of the chicken might not be a smart move in prolonging my tenure.

Government officials such as Simon are often prominent on the performative centre stage of aid – cutting ribbons at school openings, launching corporate plans and heralding yet another MoU, often in the company of a colourful troupe of *singsing* dancers. There was at least one picture of such an activity per day in the copies of the *Post Courier* that arrived in Buka on the daily flight, and I often thought that the hardest working people in all of Bougainville were those in the 20-person bamboo band hired to appear at each event.

Despite their prominence, these officials are not those who build the schools, write the plans or try to give life to signed documents. Aid delivery is contracted out, implemented by organisations that remain firmly backstage, such as the ones I worked for. These groups included

2   Australian Government Department of Foreign Affairs and Trade, 'Development Assistance in Papua New Guinea', dfat.gov.au/geo/papua-new-guinea/development-assistance/papua-new-guinea.

commercial companies, international non-governmental organisations and smaller, more boutique outfits. In the course of my years spent working in PNG and Bougainville, I was contracted to work for several such organisations and companies.

It is precarious work. In contracting terms, the Australian government is the principal and these companies their agents, with the power dynamic between them reflecting this hierarchy. Companies run on contracts, and the key determinant of success for a project can be whether those funding the project deem it a success. Accordingly, organisational incentives for contractors are yoked with the continual provision of broadly favourable information and the need to account for funds spent. A lot of effort went into presenting a cheery version of reality to people like Simon.

We had arranged this chicken lunch to discuss progress (or the lack thereof) on my assignment to facilitate the 'drawdown of powers and functions' that was spelled out in my elaborate terms of reference. While I may not have come expecting invigorated bureaucrats earnestly sharpening their pencils while I shuttled drafts, it did surprise me just how little oomph there was about the place. I was starting to feel as if my job description had been developed in a laboratory of wishful thinking.

Magical powers were ascribed to the term 'drawdown', and many Bougainville government bureaucrats would make it out to be a thoroughly seamless process – little more than 'Click your fingers and it'll happen' – but, when I pressed further, no-one actually knew what the term meant.

I explained the 'drawdown' process to Simon over our second piece of chicken, a luscious breast for him, a scrawny leg for me (*Were the Hot Rooster staff favouring him because they knew he was of importance?*). I began at the beginning, the Peace Agreement, and how the compromise over the region's political arrangements was intricate and unique in that they provide for autonomy on a progressive scale. (The design of the Peace Agreement is lauded for the sophistication of its constitutional construction.)[3] I noted how a number of governmental powers and functions were vested in the ABG upon its establishment, and how the Peace Agreement provided frameworks whereby the ABG could acquire additional powers and functions for topics as diverse as cemeteries, lotteries, health and education. Although the term 'drawdown' was

---

3   See Wolfers, 'Bougainville Autonomy'.

an evocative one, the reality of the process was mechanistic and dry. It required Bougainville to prepare a request based on the criteria laid out in the Bougainville Constitution. This request needed to focus on issues with the potential to bring about an economic dividend, and the ABG was expected to specify its resourcing needs to exercise the power or function. Moreover, the two governments were required to develop joint plans. Papua New Guinea was tasked with paying for costs for the personnel, construction and whatever else was necessary for Bougainville to exercise the new powers. Little of this had happened.

Simon asked me about the laws, which, as my earlier experience had already revealed, seemed to be the obsession of many a Bougainville bureaucrat. Recalling my attempts to discover the progress of land laws, I told him how every official appeared wed to telling me, 'What we need is a law', as if that were the just-add-water solution to every problem. Opining how this simplistic solve-all might have rung true in theory, I pointed out that the statute book was full of unimplemented laws, giving the lie to magical hopes for law as action. A plethora of legal 'solutions' from the *Inward Investment Act* (2013), which created a set of offices that were never set up, to a *Physical Planning Act* (2013) that planned not much, all evidenced that laws alone were incapable of providing a wand-waving remedy. There were, however, important exceptions to this seeming inaction. It is important to note that the ABG has successfully conducted three [now four] general elections, passed 50-plus pieces of legislation, and established its own public service structures and financial management system separate from those of PNG. The ABG had drawn down the powers over mining, developed new legislation and set up a new department for Mining and Energy Resources with World Bank support.

Fired up now by the MSG in my drumstick, I alluded to my discovery of the further obsession of bureaucrats with signing off on MoUs and extolling them as the prerequisite for everything and anything, even though, in legal terms, they amounted to little more than a gentlemen's agreement. Drafted in vague and faux-legal language, these MoUs committed the ABG and PNG government to programs of cooperation but failed to provide any of the funding needed to operationalise them. Drawing down powers via an MoU had given Bougainville a lot of 'on-paper' powers without any additional funding to give them meaningful effect. In reality, I told him with some despair, the Bougainville government assumed additional responsibilities without commensurate resourcing. This led to my explanation that a suitable analogy would be that of a driving license for a motor vehicle: via the MoUs, the ABG had been awarded a driving licence, yet was awaiting the skills needed to drive, while neither a car nor the costs of petrol had been forthcoming. I concluded by stating emphatically that it was a strange strategy: there's not much point having a driving license if you can't drive, don't have a car and have no petrol. It was administrative decoration, at best.

'There's no obvious easy way out of this, is there?' he asked. There was not; and even if there had been, it could not have been packaged into time-bound terms of reference with a clear beginning, middle and end – certainly, nothing that could easily be assembled IKEA-style or tweeted about. I shared with Simon a Tok Pisin expression I'd heard that seemed to sum up the work of the programs such as the one I was working on: *brukim bus*, translated literally as 'to cut one's way through thick bush'. I had heard it used before as a metaphor for the business of government or administration: to hack one's way through the thicket of one issue, only to find oneself immediately confronted with another piece of impenetrable foliage straight after and to have to start all over again. It is a common phrase, one adopted by Theodore Miriung, a man often regarded as a 'lost leader' of Bougainville.[4] A politician, he was assassinated during the conflict, his killers suspected to be members of the Papua New Guinea Defence Force and the Bougainville Resistance Force, a pro-PNG home guard. Another Bougainville leader, Joseph Kabui, the ABG's first president, often used the same term, brukim bus, to describe the efforts he led from 1997 onwards to find a peaceful resolution to the conflict.

To be sure, there were reportable accomplishments, but in many ways the greatest value of the support from people like me was in ensuring continuity of purpose, enabling longevity and tenacity, in simply being there and being of use for whatever problems were at hand, few of which were either grand or sweeping. The problem, however, with the muddling-through, steady-as-she-goes gospel of *brukim bus* is the lack of an obvious metric for determining value. This work was dull trudge with little fortune or glory attached and not much to announce. Between Simon and me there was also another problem, unsaid, as to what our role here was: to prepare a state-in-waiting or just to keep a part of PNG bumbling along? Australia's policy on Bougainville was a six-of-one, half-

---

4   Natalie Whiting, 'Bougainville Independence Referendum Renews Interest in Theodore Miriung Murder Mystery', ABC News, 11 December 2019, abc.net.au/news/2019-12-11/bougainville-referendum-revives-theodore-miriung-murder-mystery/11782220.

a-dozen-of-the-other, 'We'll-support-whatever-the parties-agree-to' bit of equivocation. Before the year 2000, Australian policy had been to regard Bougainville as an integral part of PNG.[5]

Did Australia really want a new Pacific neighbour? Did anyone? This was the political setting within which the program I was part of worked. However, I decided that bringing up that topic with Simon might be as impolitic as mentioning the presence of the rat that scurried across the floor.

5   For a critique of Australia's involvement in the conflict, see Kristian Lasslett, 'State Crime by Proxy: Australia and the Bougainville Conflict', *British Journal of Criminology* 52, no. 4 (2012), 705–23, doi. org/10.1093/bjc/azs012. See also R. J. May, 'The Situation on Bougainville: Implications for Papua New Guinea, Australia and the Region', *Current Issues Brief* 9 (1997), aph.gov.au/sitecore/content/ Home/About_Parliament/Parliamentary_Departments/Parliamentary_Library/Publications_Archive/ CIB/CIB9697/97cib9.

6

A trip to Port Moresby

I thought often of the canny and candid old police officer whom I had met some years back when he requested the trip to Port Moresby in my first few months in Buka. Seasoned from experience of 20-plus years of programs of support to the police funded by Australia and New Zealand, he was both fluent in donorese and honest enough to admit how he just wanted some time away from his old routine. And who could blame him? We had visited his police accommodation in the course of our visit; it had a condemned feel to it: broken windows, damp mattresses, a urinous smell rising from the floors and a drop toilet outside. Clean sheets, free internet access and an all-included breakfast buffet sounded pretty good in comparison. His request was completely rational to me. I would have done the same myself, and there were occasions on which I had. I once lived in New York, working at a think-tank writing up high-brow technocratic research intended, ostensibly, to assist places recovering from conflict, like Bougainville. It was a poorly paid position, and I would often agree to go on trips to access the per diem, money that could help defray the costs of rent and living in an expensive city. A cantankerous boss only made the wisdom of this approach more appealing. There were months in which it was the only strategy I had to pay the rent, and I dreamed up no end of reasons to be away.

It made total sense to me, therefore, that the lure of the trip (and the material benefits it provided) sometimes felt like the defining impetus behind bureaucratic decision-making. Port Moresby, the capital city of the country so many said they wanted to break away from, exerted an almost magnetic pull upon some in the government in Buka. So much energy was spent in either arranging trips to Port Moresby or trying to secure funding for a plane ticket, accommodation and the coveted travel allowance that it was a wonder other administrative tasks were given a look-in.

Going on funded trips also made sense beyond the time-honoured reason of topping up the take-home wage. Often characterised as a 'joint creation', the Peace Agreement required joint effort for it to work, and for the system of autonomy to operate and develop as intended. Meetings to hammer out joint cooperative arrangements are a familiar feature of intergovernmental relations all over the world. What always surprised me was how little appeared to come out of this cornucopia of trips. What did these meetings – the meetings everyone was so anxious to hold and attend – actually consist of?

My curiosity got the better of me, and when I was invited to go join the government on a delegation for a Joint Supervisory Body meeting, I resoundingly agreed. The Joint Supervisory Body, better known by its initials, JSB, was conceived in the Peace Agreement as a modest technical body to oversee the agreement's implementation and resolve disputes between the two governments. There was also self-interest in my wanting to attend the JSB meeting. The winnowing isolation of my new home had got to me after a few months. Some evenings I would go running alongside the airport runway towards the setting magenta sun and feel as if I was close to dropping off the end of the world. The offer of a trip to Port Moresby seemed terribly exotic by comparison. When I arrived and had a cold glass of wine at Port Moresby's Holiday Inn, I felt as full of wonder as Mick 'Crocodile' Dundee did when he first visited New York. Leaving aside my personal yearnings, however, this was also a chance to experience firsthand how things worked in practice.

Many of the files in my office related to past meetings of the JSB, and these meetings had attained sacramental importance in Buka.

What struck me when I looked through the minutes of JSB's past was how packed the agenda was every time, yet how little seemed to be accomplished. Issues were habitually punted from one meeting to the next, with public servants instructed to go away and work on issues, then report back with solutions. The fact that such activity frequently failed to materialise or result in actionable solutions did not seem to dampen the enthusiasm for repeated rounds of the same well-worn routine, and I was asked to help prepare the delegation to ensure they'd be ready to participate when the next JSB meeting occurred.

Filled with the naivety of the greenhorn, emboldened with learnings acquired in an online course in organising effective meetings, I came to help a number of other advisers to bring this meeting together. An agenda was worked up, the plan being for relevant departmental heads to develop written briefs outlining the specific issues they wanted discussed and actions they recommended, in order to focus everyone's attention on moving forward. The papers would then be compiled in a booklet to be sent to NCOBA well in advance of the meeting, the assumption being that NCOBA would by then have their own equivalent documentation, and out of all this a succinct agenda would emerge. The bureaucrats would brief the political leaders, who, in turn, would skilfully advocate and negotiate. It was a bureaucratic wet dream.

I was mugged by reality, just as many of my predecessors had been. The first challenge was how to get some people focused on the specifics rather than fussing over whether they had a room booking. The second challenge was defining the specifics. 'We must discuss the issues of fisheries before the JSB,' I would hear from the director of fisheries (total number of people in the directorate: three).

'OK, great, but what do we want to discuss? What's the position we want to take? What do we want to get out of the meeting?' Fisheries indeed seemed like a critical issue to focus on. The Peace Agreement provided for revenue-sharing between Bougainville and PNG for fish caught in the Exclusive Economic Zone associated with Bougainville. There was large money at stake – one rosy estimate, backdated to when the government was established in 2005, was as much as A$600 million[1] – although few seemed aware of this. Then, just as I was hoping my questions would

---

1   Thomas Betitis, Mahara Auhi and Richard Mounsey, Department of Primary Industries Fisheries Directorate of the Autonomous Bougainville Government, 'A Brief Outline of Bougainville's Revenue Potential from Living Aquatic Resources and Tasks Required to Be Undertaken', PowerPoint presentation, delivered at the ABG Revenue and Tax Summit, 27–29 September 2017, Buka, Autonomous Region of Bougainville, www.abg.gov.pg/images/misc/15._Fisheries_Tax_Revenue_presentation.pdf. The amount of access and licensing fees derived by PNG from the regionally administered Pacific tuna licensing scheme in 2020 was US$133.1 million (PNGK467 million). The ABG could expect to receive between 20 and 30 per cent of that amount (depending on the calculation of the percentage of PNG EEZ that is 'associated with' Bougainville territory). See Anthony J. Regan, *Criminality in Maritime Bougainville* (Vienna: UN Office on Drugs and Crime), 15.

elicit some actionable ideas, up rose the knee-jerk bureaucratic crutch: 'Um … we need to focus on signing an MoU.' (A draft document had been written in 2011 and never signed.)

Many of the papers weren't produced; those that were had the feel of having been recycled from elsewhere. In the end, fellow advisers and I wrote most of the paperwork. What should have been organised and deliberative turned out to be a last-minute scramble.

Why were the papers never written? Bureaucracies run on paper, but not all Bougainville bureaucrats were at ease with writing documents. In dealing with issues that involved financial calculations, many shared my arithmophobia, my unease with numbers. It was clear that not everyone understood the operating system of the Peace Agreement. Not being in full command of the facts and figures (and not knowing the constitutional clauses on which they are based) would put anyone in a poor position to advocate and negotiate for what one wanted out of a meeting.

Chaos of equal proportions beset the PNG side. The NCOBA printer was on the blink, lime-green paper being the only option when it was eventually coaxed back to life. The PNG side had developed a completely different agenda and no papers. What fascinated me the most was that upon discovering this snafu, no-one on the Bougainville side sought to raise an objection. Maybe I was the only one to have realised the error or to have cared. I remember feeling the words forming in my throat to point out the error and managed to stop myself. The meeting itself – all men at the table – ended after a couple of hours and was pronounced a success by all.

As I looked back at the resolutions of that meeting, I realised that they were the same issues time and again: transferring additional governmental powers, reaching agreement on financial arrears the Bougainville government claims are owed to it,[2] the sharing of revenues from fisheries. Hardy perennials then, they have persisted even to the present. As I was finishing this book in 2022, a friend sent me the agenda for the latest JSB. It looked identical to that of the JSB meeting I attended in 2016.

* * *

2   Kylie McKenna, Implementation of the *Bougainville Peace Agreement: Implications for Referendum*, PNG National Research Institute Research Report 6 (2019), 12.

I once danced the foxtrot with Queen Elizabeth, you know? I was her bodyguard when she came here in 1974. I told her all about my adventures in the Golden Triangle when trying to apprehend the drug lord Hun Sa. She was very impressed. She was a good dancer. I do wish we'd kept in touch. I liked the Duke, too. He was a bit of a lad. Liked a wine or two. Do you want a wine? It's happy hour, after all. Me, I'll stick to the juice.

I knew about Queen Elizabeth being a sassy mover because Chief Ila Geno had told me the story a couple of times before. It was one of his favourites, along with his account of how, when he was deputy commissioner, he had refused an order to deploy Police Mobile Squads to Bougainville to clear a landowner-established roadblock at Panguna.[3]

He was in his early seventies now. While a constant critic of the government, he was a hallowed eminence within Port Moresby's elite, still muscular and imposing, but with a soft face and teddy-bear eyes.

We were at the Royal Port Moresby Yacht Club, the place where an Irish writer named Beatrice Grimshaw, whose works I'd been reading, had lived in a houseboat for years in the early part of last century. Grimshaw, who wrote garish romance and adventure stories, was once spoken of in the same league as Joseph Conrad and Robert Louis Stevenson, and, probably more than any other writer, she did much to seed the idea of what is now PNG as a dark and dangerous place, a place where no travellers would want to go. Or, at least, we were close to where she would have been. Because of land reclamation, the old yacht club that had been her home was slightly farther inland these days, its clubhouse now inhabited by an Australian government program supporting the country's multitudinous law and justice agencies, a satellite office of which was in Buka. The sign outside the old building that had once blazoned their logos was weathered to the point of obsolescence, and the inside was stuffed full of old boxes of documents detailing more than two decades of initiatives, implementation plans, reviews, posters and requisition forms.

In the 'new' yacht club where we were catching up, it felt like the olden days. Sepia pictures of grizzled whitefellas adorned the walls. The head of the yacht club was called the commodore, the deputy captain sail. We were

3 For a brief account of his story about this incident, see Anthony J. Regan, 'Bougainville: Origins of the Conflict, and Debating the Future of Large-Scale Mining', in *Large-Scale Mines and Local-Level Politics: Between New Caledonia and Papua New Guinea*, ed. Colin Filer and Pierre-Yves Le Meur (Canberra: ANU Press, 2017), 353–414, doi.org/10.22459/LMLP.10.2017.

sitting outside on the deck, looking out at hundreds of boats bobbing in the marina and some joggers labouring along a dusty path behind a wire fence along the outskirts of the grounds. Ringed by a security fence, it was one of the few outside spaces in Moresby deemed safe enough to run solo without a security car trailing behind. On the table beside us, three Aussies in singlets were haggling loudly over the price of an outboard motor. It was always the place where Chief Ila Geno wanted to meet. Independent Papua New Guinea's new elite felt quite at home sitting in the chairs of old commodores. It reminded me of the time we met the old tyrant Mugabe at State House in Harare. More than two generations after both countries became independent, echoes of the colonial ambience of long ago didn't feel too far away.

My wine arrived and tasted as if a blowtorch had recently been applied to it. Ila had made the wiser choice with his orange juice. He wasn't much of a drinker, and besides, he had an official meeting to get to after ours. 'What will anyone think if I arrive smelling of wine?' he asked. The juice exemplified everything about Ila: professionalism would always trump any personal excess – that, and his underlying spine of ethics and probity. Not even for the Duke of Edinburgh was he going to let those principles drop.

By the time the royals arrived in 1974, Ila was an up-and-comer rising through the ranks of the police as the country prepared for independence the following year. I had seen some pictures of him in the newspapers: black hair, upright, sombre look, never too far from the Queen. The monarch visited in a year when everything seemed promising. Independence was a year away, and the country-to-be was flourishing with possibility. A young John Momis was leading a Parliamentary Constitutional Planning Commission and had been traversing the country, developing ideas to put into a new constitution. The founding document bespeaks an optimistic, idealised vision for the future nation, steeped as it was in liberation theology, social justice and belief in the self-actualising power of the individual. It was a long document but written with none of the vague verbosity that characterised so much contemporary government phraseology. 'The success of a nation, we believe, depends ultimately on its people and their leaders,' the framers wrote. I had written out some other quotes from the document in my notebook, among them:

No amount of careful planning in governmental institutions or scientific disciplines will achieve liberation and fulfilment of the citizens of our country unless the leaders – those who hold official positions of power, authority or influence – have bold vision, work hard and are resolutely dedicated to the service of their people.[4]

The constitution that eventually emerged from their deliberations is considered among the most comprehensive in the world. At face value, there is much that is familiar, the PNG government having inherited institutions from Australia: a parliament modelled on the Westminster system that elects a prime minister, who chairs a cabinet, which is supported by a bureaucracy. There is much that is visually familiar, too. Wigs still retain persuasive ritual power; judges and barristers sport them on their sweltering heads. The speaker of Papua New Guinea's parliament is weighed down by a thatch of horsehair of such length and weight that he resembles a Dickensian magistrate. It felt similar to those parts of Zimbabwe in which the clocks seemed to have stopped, replicating colonial administrative features that despite the heat and incongruity have always been expected to travel and be instituted intact, features that stayed long after new flags were flown.

On the face of it, the types of leadership that the founders of the PNG Constitution foresaw were rarely present. Some political leaders owned houses and share portfolios in Australia that seemed hard to square with modest parliamentary allowances.[5] The secretaries – heads of government departments – were always prominent in the newspapers, announcing one thing or another. The country clung happily to the formalisms, bureaucratese and appurtenances of old, but with little notion as to where to go next. Bougainville struck me as a facsimile, many of its own institutions mini-versions of Papua New Guinea's.

Ila's speciality through the rest of his years was to avoid doing the easy thing. He ascended to the rank of chief of police but resigned rather than follow a prime ministerial directive to make particular personnel decisions. He had been an unquiescent chief ombudsman but found it harder to find success in electoral politics. In the past two elections, he and his party had fielded a slate of candidates running on an anti-corruption

4   PNG Constitutional Planning Committee, *Report 1974*, 'Chapter 3: The Leadership Code', Pacific Islands Legal Information Institute, Paragraph 1, paclii.org/pg/CPCReport/Cap3.htm.
5   J. C. Sharman, *The Despot's Guide to Wealth Management: On the International Campaign against Grand Corruption* (Ithaca: Cornell University Press, 2017), doi.org/10.1017/s1537592718001755.

platform. Only one was successful. When I was in Buka, he was working on a number of projects, including one as a *pro bono* member of a board of inquiry for the Bougainville government. The role was prescribed in the *Bougainville Senior Appointments Act* (2014),[6] and it came with a sting: should a senior bureaucrat be referred for wrongdoing, a board of inquiry had to be formed to investigate, and its findings would be binding. Ila's first job in the role was to investigate the chief secretary, whose suspension I became aware of when I arrived. Although we didn't know it at the time, Ila would be kept busy by investigations in the years to follow. More of that later.

Too scrupulous to disclose the particulars of specific cases, he was nevertheless persuasive as to where the heart of the issue lay. For Ila, the difficulty related to the difference between what he called 'office culture' – working in a modern bureaucracy to implement technical plans based on standard systems and procedures – and 'custom culture', which was replete with a wide set of familial, religious and clan obligations, and in which leadership and authority come from acquiring resources and then distributing them. As he said, the idea of the state was new here, a house whose rooms still needed to be filled.[7]

Anthropologists chose to come here at the turn of the 20th century for their fieldwork precisely because of the effective absence of formal administration. Two dominant features emerged in their writings: one, of obligation between small groups as the glue holding these societies together, and the other the phenomenon of the *bikman* (big man – they are almost always men), where leadership is associated with the ability to acquire and duly distribute resources to followers.[8] Leadership, power and influence are accumulated or acquired through personal actions, 'public oratory, informal persuasion, and the skilful conduct of both private and public wealth exchange', rather than through diligent perusal of corporate

6   'Bougainville Senior Appointments Act 2014', Autonomous Bougainville Government, www.abg.gov.pg/uploads/acts/Act_2014-6-Bougainville_Senior_Appointments.compressed.pdf.

7   See a two-part article Ila wrote on this subject: Ila Geno, 'Governance, Ethics and Leadership in Papua New Guinea – A Personal Perspective', *Devpolicy* (blog), 1 and 22 March, 2019), devpolicy.org/author/ila-geno/.

8   Rena Lederman, 'Big Man, Anthropology of', in *International Encyclopedia of the Social & Behavioral Sciences* (Second edition), ed. James Wright (Oxford: Pergamon, 2015), 567–73.

planning documents.[9] In some of Bougainville's matrilineal societies – examples include the Nagovisi and Selau people – 'big women' are also recognised. This is not the case in most other parts of PNG.

Big men rely on personal relationships and access to resources to establish obligation and fealty. Leadership is fluid; this is not a context in which a big man can rest on his laurels. Forever looking warily over his shoulder lest he be trumped by another, it is imperative that the big man continue to amass and distribute resources, for it is only through this process that political power can continue. These rules of the game – driving action through relationships and the distribution of resources as fundamental blocks of political power – characterise Papua New Guinea's politics, notwithstanding the formal edifices of the received Westminster system and bureaucracy modelled on that of Australia. In the evocative phrasing of Francis Fukuyama:

> It takes only a couple of hours to fly from Port Moresby to Cairns or Brisbane, but in that flight, one is in some sense traversing several thousand years of political development[10]

Hard to construct a governance plan adhering to neat timetables out of this. Toggling between these two cultures – and navigating the obligations and often conflicting values of each – was challenging for bureaucrats, politicians and aid workers alike. Even fluent second-language speakers find it easier to revert to their first language. Ila was a man with an unbounded faith in rules, policies and procedures. His bureaucratic career showed its possibilities and its limits. His political career, and the nosedive it took, showed its limits more than anything and brought to mind the endeavour we were engaging in. As George Orwell wrote: 'To see what is in front of one's nose needs a constant struggle.'[11] No wonder it was easier to think of things in terms of long-range plans than to try to acknowledge the very different rules of the political games going on right in front of us, rules we as outsiders scarcely understood.

---

9   Lederman, 'Big Man'.
10   Francis Fukuyama, *The Origins of Political Order* (Sydney: Allen & Unwin, 2011), xv.
11   George Orwell, 'In Front of Your Nose', The Orwell Foundation, orwellfoundation.com/the-orwell-foundation/orwell/essays-and-other-works/in-front-of-your-nose/.

PART TWO

Many had no proud ideas.
— Bougainvillean academic and
novelist Regis Tove Stella

7

The road to Arawa

At what felt like each kilometre of the bony road of yellowed dust from Buka Town towards Panguna and the old capital of Arawa, Eddie Mohin pointed out vanished landmarks of the Bougainville conflict. Imperceptible to my eye, they were as real to him as the navy-blue University of Oxford cap on his head. This is the part of the road where a helicopter strafed us; this is where there was once a defence force post that we attacked in the dead of night; this is where one of our comrades was shot; this is where we captured this person; this is where I kidnapped the man who is now the region's president; this is where I played the guitar and sang with the peacekeepers who came after the ceasefire; and there, over to the mountains, far away, beyond lie the two rivers where the tailings swept out to sea.[1]

'Tailings' is a word I had not heard before I went to Bougainville. It is a polite term for the sludgy and toxic by-product of mining operations. More than a billion tonnes of such slag were dumped into two of Bougainville's rivers – the Jaba and the Kawerong – during the 17 years of the Panguna mine's operations.[2] It killed off the fish[3] and the river crocodiles, and

---

1   M. J. F. Brown, 'A Development Consequence – Disposal of Mining Waste in Bougainville, Papua New Guinea', *Geoforum* 18 (1974): 19–27; Don Vernon, 'The Panguna Mine', in *Bougainville before the Conflict,* ed. Anthony J. Regan and Helga M. Griffin (Canberra: ANU Press, 2015), 258–73, doi.org/10.22459/BBC.08.2015.
2   'Porphyry copper and gold ore body contains very low percentages of ore, and so ore-bearing rock has to be crushed to a powder by several "ball mills" of balls of successively smaller diameter, before chemical processes extract a concentrate of close to 30 per cent metal, which is sent to the coast by a pipeline for export for processing, leaving vast amounts of discarded fine waste, all tipped into the river system.' (Anthony Regan, email message to author, March 2022).
3   Applied Geology Associates Ltd, *Environmental, Socio-economic and Public Health Review of Bougainville Copper Mine, Panguna* (New Zealand: Applied Geology Associates Ltd, 1989).

created a moonscape of silted high banks, along with a massive, toxic delta in the ocean at the mouth of the Jaba River. Sores, skin disorders, continual gastric problems and high rates of miscarriage remain to this day as grim legacies of the tailings.[4]

Eddie drove one of the big yellow 10-wheel haul trucks at the mine and, later, was a commander in the BRA. He became a member of the team that negotiated the Peace Agreement and, subsequently, a member of the commission that developed Bougainville's constitution. A poet, a guitarist, sometimes an evangelical preacher, he was reputed to have been a bit of a hellraiser back in the day. Eddie wore an array of hats and baseball caps so frequently that I was always surprised when on rare occasions he took one off to reveal a shiny, bald head.

Eddie's life was more serene now. He and his wife Fidelma tended their 'gardens' – a patch of land in a clearing of jungle with coconuts, taro and green vegetables, a few kilometres walk up a steep mountain path from their house. He ran for parliament a couple of times but never had the money required to secure the votes. He was in his fifties but still sinewy, a person of clear stature and authority. If any problems arose in Buka or surrounds, the police would call Eddie, not because they suspected him of any involvement, but because his moral authority and reach outweighed their own. Sometimes he did odd jobs for the Bougainville government, for which he was rarely paid, out of a sense of duty to his long-gestating nation.

I had met Eddie at one of the workshops at the Lands Office, and we'd spent some weekends walking in Buka Island. We would start near his village, passing through overgrown plantations, past stones, trees, and markers that carried meanings to his clan, towards little knotted tree shelters high up on the mountain slopes and waterfalls, places where he said the spirits gathered at night. He'd go immediately before me on our perambulations, bush knife in hand, thwacking away bush and carving out little steps in the jungle floor to help me down vertiginous descents

---

4   Keren Adams and Hollie Kerwin, *After the Mine: Living with Rio Tinto's Deadly Legacy* (Melbourne: Human Rights Law Centre, 2020), static1.squarespace.com/static/580025f66b8f5b2 dabbe4291/t/5e7d7cce47c7f816da86005f/1585282297310/AfterTheMineRioTintoDeadlyLegacy. pdf; Denoon, *Under the Skin*; J. Dove, T. Miriung and M. Togolo, 'Mining Bitterness', in *Problem of Choice: Land in Papua New Guinea's Future*, ed. Peter G. Sack, (Canberra: Australian National University Press, 1974), 181–89; Kylie McKenna, *Corporate Social Responsibility and Natural Resource Conflict* (Abingdon-on-Thames: Routledge, 2016), 26.

that would dissolve with the next rains. These walks were frequently challenging. Once we went with the 'tax and revenue' adviser and feared he would not be able to deliver on his efforts to improve the government's dire revenue position because the challenge of ascending an acclivitous, muddied mountain slope threatened to provoke in him a massive heart attack.

Eddie's village was Kahule, located about 20 kilometres from Buka Town over scrabbled, holed and jagged stone that formed part of the 'Buka Island ring road'. It was a village of about 100 bush huts made from wood, palm and rattan, and a school painted red with no books and no windows, but with small signs atop the doors overwritten with words emanating from another era, such as 'common room' and 'duty prefect'. In the village hall, handwritten organisational charts for various village committees were on display, all of which Eddie appeared to sit on.

We passed through the rusting detritus of the Second World War on our walks: bits of tanks, cylinders, aeroplane propellers. Eddie said his father remembered the flashes and noise as the planes roared overhead. Before all the armies left after the armistice in 1945, soldiers buried much of their armaments into the soft ground at Torokina, off the west coast, and abandoned incapacitated vehicles right where they had stopped. When seeking to arm himself for his war, Eddie and his contemporaries had asked their fathers where the machine guns, rifles and pistols were hidden and dug them up, using mechanical know-how acquired from the mine to repurpose turrets from downed planes, and bits of metal, into weapons. The samurai swords the Japanese left behind proved useful for both ceremonial adornment on the rare occasion that a journalist came visiting, and for close-quarters lancing.

Visiting Kahule provided me with a reality check on life in Bougainville – its precarity, its obligations and its costs. This was an expensive place, even by Australian standards. A round trip on the rattletrap cattle truck that people stood in to get into Buka each day cost the equivalent of A$5–10. No-one was rich by any conventional standards, and people spent their days up the mountain with bush knives, tending their gardens. Everyone wore second-hand clothing. I'd pass Eddie some money for his guiding, but no matter how much it was, it felt insubstantial and never enough to cover the expenses of his life.

Eddie came into town a few days each week, either cramming himself into the rattletrap truck that bumped and ground its way through the craters on his road or catching a banana boat. We would meet up at '*Ralph's kai bar*' for a meat pie, chicken and sweet potato chips. He'd talk about how he was going to do some security work for the government. I'd ask him if he'd been paid for the previous work.

I felt for Eddie. He was a talented man, and his story of dashed potential and sputters of paid work was commonplace. There were too many men like Eddie in modern-day Bougainville, men who spent day after idle day with too little to do, scrawny reward for years of conflict and dedication to the singing flame. If anything, the generation younger than his were in an even more wretched state. I'd see many of them every day in Buka. The clothes they wore were vintage cast-offs from Australia and elsewhere, bearing images of rugby league teams, Baywatch stars, a young Kylie Minogue, forgotten political campaigns for local councils and national office. I once saw a young man wearing a red 'Kevin '07' T-shirt, the Kevin being Kevin Rudd, twice prime minister of Australia, the ''07' referring to 2007, the year Rudd won a federal election for the first time. The young folk would loll up and down the main drag, standing underneath the awnings of shops to snatch some shade, eyes deadened. These walkers up and down are known by the shorthand of the 'lost generation',[5] an entire swathe of the population who missed their schooling because of the Crisis. While referenced frequently as a problem, there are so many of them that it is hard to know what to do with them. They are like one of Bougainville's volcanoes: smouldering.

I was curious to see Arawa, and Eddie had offered to be my guide. I relished trips like this, as they made me feel more alive than being in the office, and I presumed Eddie was glad of a break from the usual routine. We had crossed over on the one-car ferry from Buka Island that morning and headed down the road. The ferryboat was painted gun-steel grey and had once been a landing craft used by the Papua New Guinean army during the Crisis. It was called the *Buka Babe*, and on it the fresh, cobalt-coloured flag of Bougainville, with the distinctive *upe* at its centre, flapped in the breeze.

---

5   Kylie McKenna et al., 'The Bougainville Referendum through the Eyes of the "Lost Generation": Observations from Siwai', *Asia Pacific Viewpoint* 62, no. 2 (2021): 193–205, doi.org/10.1111/apv. 12300.

We passed an abandoned coconut plantation, and I asked Eddie about his grandfather, 'Kerosene', who had once worked as a manservant there. 'Kerosene' wasn't his real name; a white man had given him the moniker, a bastardisation of 'Tsorohin', the name of the village on Buka Island from which he hailed. The white man was called Robert Stuart. He had arrived in Bougainville in the 1920s and stayed here for 40 years. Stuart wrote a vigorous account of his japes and antebellum attitudes as a copra plantation manager and owner in a memoir entitled *Nuts to You* (1977).[6] It evokes a distinct time-capsule quality of the era in which Eddie grew up, when strict separation between the races prevailed and whites in white suits ran the roost, applying an approach to people-management that could be characterised as: 'Don't give them too much for Christmas because it'll only make them soft.'

Are things really that much different now in independent Papua New Guinea?

Dual pay and conditions between expatriate and nationals has been a perpetual issue across many sectors in PNG. Scholars have identified as much as a 9:1 gap between salaries, a ceiling described as 'more like concrete than glass'.[7] In the last decade, cracks in this ceiling have emerged in other traditionally 'expat' prominent industries such as mining and accounting. Yet, in development, wage imbalance seems harder to shift.

Away from Bougainville, I would co-research an academic article that explored the experiences of men – both 'local' and 'international' – who work or have worked in the development sector in PNG.[8] Their multiple narratives showed how a combination of pay variations, different cultural vantage points, and bureaucratic dynamics left both constituencies feeling inconsequential, diminished and disempowered. Decades on from the time of Eddie's father, there may be more similarities than we would like to believe, including in the industry in which I was working.

I had been behind the steering wheel so far, but Eddie suggested that he drive over the torrent at Aita, which was about the halfway point of the three-hour drive. I was happy to give up the driver's seat. He had

6   Robert Stuart, *Nuts to You!* (Sydney: Wentworth Books, 1977).
7   S.C. Carr et al., 'International–Local Remuneration Differences across Six Countries: Do They Undermine Poverty Reduction Work?', *International Journal of Psychology* 45 (2010): 321–40.
8   Gordon Peake and Ceridwen Spark, 'Australian Aid in Papua New Guinea: Men's Views on Pay Disparities, Power Imbalances and Written Products in the Development Sector', *The Australian Journal of Anthropology* 32, no.1 (2021): 3–18, doi.org/10.1111/taja.12387.

more experience in circumnavigating river crossings than I did; besides, having him at the wheel meant there was less chance we'd be accosted for fees for the crossing. The bridge spanning the river had collapsed some time previously, and now men gathered on either side demanding money, although it was not exactly clear to me what service they were providing. The leader of these opportunistic men had the oddest of *nom de plumes* it is possible to conceive of. His given name was Laurence, but he luxuriated in the nickname of 'The Black Pussy', which indicated he was either a supremely confident fellow or not across the finer subtleties of idiomatic English. The man himself wasn't there that day, and we were waved through by three inebriates wearing T-shirts of, respectively, Iron Maiden, Slayer and Rage Against the Machine.

'They think all white people have plenty of money,' said Eddie, 'and you've always come here to take our riches.' It seemed impossible to escape one's skin colour here, and there was certainly enough recent history to support such a view: the prospectors and fortune-hunters who flocked to Bougainville to search for gold,[9] and the planters who came to try their luck at making money from coconuts and cocoa, were only the beginning.

The gold and copper discovered in the early 1960s on Bougainville Island were found near Panguna, in the mountains of central Bougainville, about 15 kilometres from the coast and a one-day upward slog through thick jungle. To bring roads to a roadless jungle, helicopters ferried parts of bulldozers for assemblage onsite, along with diamond-tipped drills forged to burrow deep into the precipitous slopes. What was found exceeded the highest expectations: it was among the largest bodies of copper ore in the world. To extract the copper required shifting 11 million cubic metres of land and the creation of a road descending steeply from the cloud-covered mountain to the coast in a place where most villagers had never even seen a car, let alone earthmovers. Helicopters whirred and bulldozers clanked, as tradies drawn from all over the world dug the pit and paved what was named the 'alpine road'.

---

9   'There were some successful artisanal mining sites, mainly pre-WWII, at Kupei, Punkuam (now Panguna) and Atamo. The Catholic Bishop of Brisbane was the main investor in the Kupei operations. In the years leading up to WWII, even very heavy rock crushing machinery was used in gold mining. It was transported by hand up to Kaupei – and it's still there. But the pickings were always lean, and as a result there was never a gold rush.' (Anthony J. Regan, email message to author, March 2022).

The initial residents of Arawa were predominantly men, many of them roistering, trailblazer types. Through some dogged internet searching, I met up with a post-war German immigrant to Australia now living near a riverbend close to the coast south of Sydney, in a house with wooden panels, a walled library of VHS videos and the faint odour of Old Spice.[10] He had been an accountant for Bechtel, the company responsible for building the town and the infrastructure, and when I met him he had been running a website for a while, putting up pictures from the early days. The frequency of the posts is slowing now: many of the old hands are in their seventies and dying off, some from the skin cancer occasioned by melanomas on their back, the result of too much swimming and beach cricket out in the remorseless, beating tropical sun.

His tales of the 1970s and 1980s were Rabelaisian, and he told them with a brio that he thought he'd lost. He told of drunken games of snakes and ladders, in which as much as a month's wages could be staked on the outcome; competitions for who could string together the longest posy of ring-pulls from beer cans, and something called a beer snake made from plastic vessels – all epic tales of drinking. It was no small wonder that anything was accomplished at all. The men had nicknames like 'Stretchy', 'Spud' and 'Chopper'. Many sported droopy moustaches; in some cases these were paired with amply sized guts. At least a few seemed to be fleeing the complications of personal lives elsewhere. This man's name was Peter, and his English was perfect, but he reflected on the fact that so many of the Australians in Arawa had been unable to read or write in English. Many were recent immigrants from non-English-speaking parts of Europe, and the complex engineering instructions they were given had to be delivered through pantomime-style miming actions. In the early days it would have been a place of not insignificant heterosexual frustration. There were approximately 10,000 men and 10 single women at the mine site during the construction phase. The single men lived in small convertible huts plastered with self-waxed pictures from *Playboy* magazine.

The newcomers brought old grudges with them. When the ecologist Richard West visited Arawa in 1970, two years before the mine opened, he wrote in his book *River of Tears* that many of the Australians there had come directly from then-Yugoslavia and divided themselves along Serb

---

10   Old Spice is a brand of men's skin and hair products popular in Australia.

and Croat lines.[11] His account of a Sunday morning in the Arawa of that time is vivid: broken beer bottles, crushed beer cans and Bougainvillean children who were heading for a choral festival being followed around by braying construction workers. 'How can you expect the native (sic) to have any respect for us?' an Australian engineer lamented to West.[12]

Arawa was designed and built according to the idealised image of an Australian country town, which was tempting to the company executives, miners and business owners, and their families. It had wide boulevards, playing fields, squash courts, a swimming pool, a golf course, a public library, an interdenominational church, a Masonic temple, a choice of hair salons and cinemas, and the largest supermarket in PNG. At the time of its completion, the output of the new thermal power station equalled twice the total amount of electricity generated throughout the rest of PNG. This was tropical adventure with flared trousers, refrigeration and all the creature comforts.

Prominent visitors came from far and wide. Queen Elizabeth and family (including honeymooners Princess Anne and Captain Mark Phillips) visited on the Royal Yacht *Britannia* in 1974. The wharf was lowered by 12 inches (30 centimetres) to save the royal party the exertion of having to step down from their launch onto the shore, and a wooden lavatory seat was flown in by special charter the day before because the one in the guest room where the Queen and the Prince were to stay was found to have a crack in it. Prince Philip drove up to the mine himself in a Land Rover via the recently laid alpine-grade road.

Writers lived in and visited Arawa. Nancy Curtis wrote a book for young readers set in Bougainville and sponsored by the company about the adventures of a boy called Little Chimbu.[13] (In *Little Chimbu in Bougainville*, the boy is rescued by the company helicopter after falling into a slurry pit.) Hammond Innes, a Scottish adventure–thriller writer whose books I'd once borrowed from my local library, also showed up a year after that book was published, seeking inspiration. All Innes's books were set in lands that to a child raised in rural Northern Ireland seemed impossibly exotic and distant. His books brought him fame, and his approach was to parlay his renown to secure an all-expenses trip and then

---

11   Richard West, *River of Tears: The Rise of the Rio Tinto Zinc Mining Corporation* (London: Earth Island Ltd, 1972), 123.

12   West, *River of Tears*, 124.

13   Nancy Curtis, *Little Chimbu in Bougainville* (Sydney: Pacific Publications, 1973).

structure a story around the visit. I don't recall reading his book set in Bougainville when I was younger, but it made for eerie reading when I read it during my time there. Entitled *Solomons Seal* and published in 1980, its plot revolved around how the untold riches of the mine uncorked the elements for a shifting and shapeless conflict.[14] Part of the book was set on Sohano, the little island that was my Bougainville home. The novel's character list included British mercenaries who arrived in Bougainville with weapons hidden and seeking access to the islands' resources. When published, reviewers deemed it diverting but far-fetched, yet most of his outlandish plot would turn out to be presciently clairvoyant. Innes's fictional mercenaries, however, were more successful than their real-world counterparts.

By the time Innes visited Bougainville, Arawa had settled into its rhythms. The Australian expats brought caricatured names from British colonies they aspired to recreate. The strip of coast where the sailing club was located was known as 'Happy Valley'. It was a town of resolutely bourgeois pursuits. There was a country club, a Lions Club and clubs for squash, golf, cricket, diving, darts, pottery, jazz and every other conceivable hobby. The Returned Services League (RSL), with its 'Cork and Fork' restaurant, was one of the most humming places in town. There was a penchant for theme nights, such as the Guy Fawkes ball over at the RSL ('Come dressed for plenty of arson around'), and the Elizabethan-themed, knees-up New Year's Eve bash at the Davara hotel, complete with a picture of a headless Tudor queen in a halter-neck top carrying her own bonce. Food was reassuringly bland. 'Nothing will be too hot and spicy!' assured the advertisement accompanying the 'Mexican fiesta'. Santa Claus would arrive to the kids' Christmas party in the mining company's helicopter to enact the same gift-dispensing ritual Veronica Hatutasi would one day have to dissuade her crying children from longing for. A short boat ride away from Arawa was the holiday island of Arovo, with its beach bar, nightclub, tennis courts and helicopter landing pad.

Families lived in the centre of town in purpose-built houses, while the single men lived in small convertible huts dotted around. Roles were disaggregated by gender. Sporting either tight-at-the-crotch shorts and knee socks or bellbottom trousers, the men would jump into Volkswagen vans and head off to work. Their partners – big hair and make-up

---

14   Hammond Innes, *Solomons Seal* (London: William Collins, 1980).

liquifying in the heat – held a dazzling array of coffee mornings. Once a month there was a women's discussion group, where topics for debate included: 'Can married women have men friends?' The employees of the mine were earning more money than they could have dreamed of back in Australia. There was so much money sloshing around that unscrupulous real estate agents would come up from Australia to swindle people into buying blocks of land on floodplains there.

Arawa and its surroundings was not just home to white expatriates. Men from elsewhere in PNG arrived to take up jobs at the mine. The Bougainvilleans called them 'redskins' because their skin was more brown in hue than their own deep black skin.[15] My colleague and friend George was one of the newcomers. He had returned to Arawa for a funeral the year before my visit, the first time he had visited in more than 40 years. Seeing the town now, and comparing it to what it was in his heyday, saddened him immensely.

The picture that emerges of Arawa at its peak is of a boozy and good-natured place with varying levels of gaucheness, hijinks and poorly disguised marital affairs. For the Australians, this was as deeply insular and intolerant of difference as any small town in Australia of its time. A friend of mine lived in Arawa as a little girl, and her childhood memories included seeing adults getting steadily more and more smashed at weekend parties while she and her brother grew fidgety and tired, waiting for the grown-ups to finish with their merrymaking and drunk-drive home. I tried to contact some of the Australians who had lived in Arawa at that time. Many of them didn't want to talk to me, as was their prerogative. One explained that my inquiries were bringing back too many happy memories that had long since been wrenched away. 'One weekend we were playing golf, and a few weeks later we were being evacuated,' another said, poignantly. Many struggled to return to living in reduced financial circumstances when they went home, and a fair few found it hard to find work again. Arawa was an irrecoverable time. I was curious to see what remained.

---

15   Jonathan Friedlaender, 'Why Do the People of Bougainville Look Unique? Some Conclusions from Biological Anthropology and Genetics', in *Bougainville before the Conflict*, ed. Anthony J. Regan and Helga M. Griffin (Canberra: ANU Press, 2015), 57–70, doi.org/10.22459/BBC.08.2015; Nash and Ogan, 'Red and Black'.

8

Town of ghosts

Eddie and I had been rattling along for a few hours by now, passing faded signs extolling road-building partnerships. We came to a fishtail in the road. To the right was Panguna, where we'd go the next day, and to the left was Arawa. We drove past some thick bushes. Eddie remembered this as a place where he had once crashed a motorbike before the conflict, after an evening of carousing. A few minutes later we arrived in the town itself, parts of which evoked elegiac feelings. Its wide boulevards still dominated, and faded whitewashed buildings with an identifiably seventies feel gave the impression of being almost ready for their former residents to return. There was a clearly painted sign to a fish-and-chip shop and forecourts to abandoned petrol stations coated in vintage regalia of Shell and Mobil. Signs remained for Australian banks that had long since closed. Pocked around walls were fading advertisements for Winfield cigarettes and for Pepsi, which proclaimed itself 'the choice of a new generation', the slogan of an advertising campaign from 1986.

But this was no ghost town. Local families were living now in the former mineworkers' houses, and the market bustled, filled with vegetables, fruit, smoked fish and beach towels bearing the names of resorts in nearby Solomon Islands. Part of old Arawa had been repurposed; the squash courts in the centre of town made for ideal trade stores. There were noticeable queues outside some establishments. One was outside the ATM at the bank, another at an ice-cream parlour, but the biggest was outside a little green-tea-coloured storefront with a handwritten sign saying 'Gold Assayer', another term of metallurgy that I wasn't familiar with before going to Bougainville. It refers to someone who tests metals for quality.

Beyond the town centre were little more than evocations. The jungle had reclaimed the golf course save for a small concrete island on which stood a small urinal block. Gobbled up entirely by the foliage were the pillars of a structure Eddie thought was once the site of the town's Masonic temple. 'We found some really strange stuff in there,' he said, reinforcing my suspicion of the Freemasons borne of an Irish Catholic childhood. We went looking for the writer Nancy Curtis's house, which was on the outskirts of town, but it, too, had been swallowed.

Down at the coast, at Kieta, all that remained of the sailing club at Happy Valley was a rusted swing gate. Of the sub-aqua club there was just the stencilling on a metal sign pointing directions to where it had once been. All the buildings in Happy Valley, including the yacht club, had been carted away by villagers, who used the material to build their own houses. The house of the provincial premier was nothing more than a few rusted girders. The concrete structure at the Davara hotel, site of the Elizabethan New Year's Eve celebrations, remained, its centrepiece swimming pool filled with grungy green water, over which a swarm of mosquitoes buzzed. Squatters were occupying many of the rooms, and the hotel's walls were daubed with graffiti depicting guns, devil masks and the pained expression on the face of what looked like a man being taken from behind. Over at the port of Loloho, we found the detritus of rusted diggers, warehouses, pipes, a metal concentrator, bits of loading trucks, copper wire, nails and brackets. Still intact was the nozzle of the pipe that would have connected into the ship's tank to send the copper concentrate overseas.

In the stretch of water where once the Royal Yacht *Britannia* had moored floated a rust bucket, tilting precariously, its white, blue and red flag slumped precipitously to one side. Sitting under the trees onshore were disconsolate and emaciated Filipinos who exuded the air of forlorn castaways, which was, in effect, what they were. They'd come here months ago at the invitation of a local member of parliament to work on a fishing project but hadn't been paid. They had run out of money and were surviving off charity from the local church. A project trajectory of such ilk was not uncommon. Bougainville has four seats in the national parliament of PNG, and its MPs were given set sums of roughly A$3 million per annum, which they were mostly free to use as they saw fit for 'district service improvements'. The fishing scheme was not unusual: the newspapers were full of similar such schemes that were invariably launched with promises of great potential windfalls. The fish that the

Filipinos caught, so the argument went, would by some unspecified means lead to an unquantifiable but always humungous quantum of wider economic progress. Like so many projects, this one hadn't panned out as 'planned'.[1]

'You came on that boat?' I asked, believing them but incredulous that the vessel in front of us could have ventured safely over any meaningful stretch of water.

'Yes, sir,' one of the men replied. 'But now the engine is not working, no parts are available, and we are here under this tree.' The MP and members of his retinue who had sponsored the initiative wasn't returning their calls. 'Do you have any food?' We drove off and brought back a few wan sausage rolls from one of the trade stores. (A few months later, the Philippines Embassy in Port Moresby would arrange to pay for the men's repatriation.)

We hired a small, motorised boat known locally as a banana boat to take us over to Arovo Island, that weekend getaway for the diving set, with tennis courts and the helicopter landing pad. Our skipper was a teenager with a tie-dyed shirt bearing the words 'sex police'. He wore one thong on his right foot, and the Jackie Onassis-style sunglasses he toted had but one arm. 'Half of what it once was' was an appropriate theme for our destination. Much of the jetty at Arovo on which had once stood hip-swaying girls in grass skirts to welcome revellers ashore (as per the promotional material) had crumbled into the sea. The old social club was a half-walled ruin. It was another place where, again, only another durable urinal remained. We stood on a concrete slab the size of two double beds, which Eddie thought was the club's old dance floor. He looked wistful. Given the conflict that followed, I had initially thought Eddie's memories of Arawa would be reminiscent of accounts of life in apartheid-era South Africa or the Deep South of the United States. But it wasn't so.

Sure, he did mention that there were those among the expats who, hands-on-hips, would shout racial epithets at him and fellow mineworkers, but many of his memories were of good times chasing women of all shades here at the Arovo holiday resort. He remembered Arawa largely as a carefree time where there was plenty of food, money and merriment – in

---

1   See Sebastian Hakalits, 'Small Scale Fishing Project Initiated', *Post Courier*, 27 October 2016, postcourier.com.pg/small-scale-fishing-project-initiated/.

all, an Arcadia of the South Pacific. He wasn't the only one. For many in modern-day Bougainville, the old Arawa was like a compass reading of the town to which people wanted to return.

A group of men arrived minutes after us; someone had called to tell them that a white man had chartered a boat, and they came with the intention of demanding arrival fees. Eddie waved them off. The combination of ruined architecture and default distrustfulness of white skins, simultaneously desperate and grasping, seemed to perfectly encapsulate the pensive sadness that cast a pall over so much of Bougainville.

Despite it all, there was certainly industry and activity on Arovo. That Sunday morning, even though it was early, we found about five people hacking away at the jungle with bush knives. Emerging out of this jungle like a modern-day Ben Gunn came a man who introduced himself as Bruce. He was a New Zealander, part Maori, part Irish, his body heavily tattooed. The designs were predominantly of Pacific origin, except for one on his right arm of two Kalashnikovs meeting at their tips, akin to the hastily devised coat of arms of a tin-pot Marxist liberation insurgency.

Bruce said he had returned home. Born in New Zealand, he had grown up on a cocoa plantation a little north of Arawa during the times of the mine and had found it hard to adjust when he moved back to New Zealand. He ran away from the family home, worked first as a farm labourer, then joined the New Zealand Army. He was demobbed and found work as a military contractor, fighting his way through Libya, Syria and Somalia. While in Mogadishu, he and his team (a Frenchman who had by then revealed himself as an outright charlatan, an Australian cop who didn't seem to know one end of a rifle from another, and a fellow Kiwi who did) found themselves pinned down in an ambush. Fearing they would lose their lives, he rang his children on the satellite phone, convinced this would be the last time they would speak. The thoughts he believed would be his last were of Bougainville, of the calm of the plantation, of waters the colours of opal and lapis lazuli, and the mists that shrouded the high mountains of the Crown Prince Range.

Something clicked in Bruce, and he was determined to get back. In the middle of the night, they made their escape, crawling out over the beach into the sea and floating down shore to emerge near the UN compound, where they found sanctuary. He quit his job soon after, and his next stop was Bougainville, where he was trying to project-manage the dream of making Arova Island a resort location once again, this time without the colonial and faintly racialist overtones of earlier days.

He had been busy. He and a small team had cleared the bush around the social club and were chopping out the thick knots of foliage around the accommodation blocks (where the structure and a few of the toilet bowls were intact, one containing a freshly dispatched poo). I could see their vision: the bar and grill would serve cold beer and fish fetched straight from the waters around the island. Their plan was for this to be the sort of place where large cruise ships could dock for food and trinkets, and tip handsomely for *singsing* performances. It was slow work, the hardest part being getting the local chiefs together to agree on a course of action and tempering their expectations that this little venture was going to make outsized profits immediately. Bruce seemed a man entirely content with himself and the life choices he had made. I envied his sense of purpose and activity, because I experienced many days in Bougainville sitting around the administration where I felt that I had much less. He was surprised by the number of visitors he had, former mineworkers and their families making pilgrimage back to Arovo. They would point to where their favourite barstool was located and recount their old carouses. The boatload of spontaneous rent-seekers we had met on our arrival showed that achieving this vision would be tough work.

* * *

We were the only guests in the Arawa Traveller's Inn that night. The rooms were pleasant, if bare, and the upstairs bar was of a good enough elevation to catch a wisp of breeze as the sun went down. We ordered dinner, beef in black bean sauce, rice and a few bottles of SP beer to wash it down with.

Eddie spoke about the prospects of an independent Bougainville. The vote was drawing close, and he was confident it would be a thumping majority for independence. Bougainville's current halfway-house political arrangements had delivered little, and better times were ahead. He was bullish, his argument similar to one advanced by most Bougainville leaders: 'We have cocoa, we have fisheries, we have gold and we have copper,' they would say. 'Bougainville is far better off without Papua New Guinea.' And without independence, what had they been fighting for?

Eddie was spot-on when it came to Bougainville's ample natural resources. There was copper and gold in the hills above us worth an estimated A$60 billion,[2] and Bougainville sat slap-bang within some of the richest waters for tuna fish in the world. As much as I wanted to embrace Eddie's optimism, my internal reality check resurfaced unbidden: what the place didn't have was a functioning administration that could deal with the complexities of resources management and of using the revenue generated to fund hospitals, schools and roads. Sometimes I felt there was an almost hallucinatory quality to these conversations about independence. Eddie and the others could see something tangible and thought it so easy to do, whereas before my eyes it was all a blur.

I woke early the next morning and went for a jog before the heat became too intense, speeding up whenever I passed groups of inebriates drinking beer and home brew, and swaying to the sounds of death metal emanating from the tinny speakers on their mobile phones. In most cases I was ignored in a good-natured sort of way, but sometimes, after running about 20 metres past them, I'd hear 'White man!' and a chorale of guttural laughs that followed. I didn't feel threatened, but it reinforced how much my skin colour carried clear and sullen associations in this little town. Unlike Buka, or anywhere else I'd been in PNG, this town also had no Chinese trade stores or shops. Local Bougainvilleans had chased them out. Of their autonomous government there was no sign, but of this being a town in a Bougainville nation there was no question.

After breakfast, we went to the park where the Peace Agreement was signed in 2001. The signatories had been carried aloft on bamboo chairs to the signing ceremony through what was by then a ruined place. It was quiet that morning, just a few drunks sleeping it off under the shade of a metal piece of public art in the shape of a globe, which reminded me of the lakeside sculpture in Canberra that marks the various voyages of Captain Cook. On this globe, the entirety of the Americas had been torn off. We then drove out past Arawa's airport to look for General Sam Kauona, one of Eddie's colleagues from the Crisis, but he wasn't at his home on the beach. He must be off on another film shoot, I speculated with a grin. A few years previously, Sam had played a starring role in a Discovery Channel series about an Alaskan family who travelled to Bougainville to

---

2   Joshua Mcdonald, 'Will Bougainville reopen the Panguna Mine?', *The Diplomat*, 22 November 2019, thediplomat.com/2019/11/will-bougainville-reopen-the-panguna-mine/.

find gold. Entitled *The Legend of Croc Gold*,[3] the series unfolded like the plot of a Shirley Conran novel, reinforcing the image of PNG as a place where the jungle drums beat and a large broth of bones is on the boil. Sam hammed it up in the role of wily chief. No gold was found, and the family departed empty-handed and empty-pocketed. It was fun to compare and contrast the daft confection on TV with the reality. The show presented the family as living in a jungle camp when they actually lived in the Traveller's Inn's competitor hotel, the Gold Dust.

On to Panguna, and an encounter with two old men on duty at the Morgan Junction checkpoint, which comprised an assemblage of metal cast-offs from the mine site itself, including a 'DANGER – KEEP OUT' sign filched from the old explosives stores. The men were in charge of a rusted boom gate at the beginning of the turnoff to the alpine road; the barrier was down, and it was clear it wasn't going to be raised until we paid what one of the men described in Tok Pisin to Eddie as '200 kina white man' fee (about A$80 at the time) and to me, in English, as a 'peacebuilding facilitation charge'. The money, he dissembled, would be put to various community goodwill projects, and when he issued the receipt, he labelled his exaction as a 'no-go zone entry tax for foreigners'. The receipt was issued in the name of the 'Kingdom of Papaala' – which, in tangible terms, consisted of not much more than the checkpoint itself. A certain Noah Musingku,[4] who called himself King David Peii II of Papaala – named after President Momis's forefather – ran this 'kingdom'. This was a man who had once presided over a pyramid scheme that ensnared many residents of Port Moresby. He lived to the south and wore, it was said, a crown smithed from Macedonian gold. This 'king' issued his own currency from a printing press once guarded by Fijian mercenaries. He made government out to be so magical that it required no work. A journalist from the Australian Broadcasting Corporation (ABC) filed a story that when he'd once visited the self-anointed king, he found him typing on a computer unconnected to any power-source.[5]

3   *The Legend of Croc Gold*, Discovery, discovery.com/shows/the-legend-of-croc-gold.
4   John Cox, 'Prosperity, Nation and Consumption: Fast Money Schemes in Papua New Guinea', in *Managing Modernity in the Western Pacific* (Brisbane: University of Queensland Press, 2011), 173.
5   Liam Fox, 'Bougainville's Conman "King" Still on the Run as Island Edges Closer to Independence' ABC News, 15 November 2020, abc.net.au/news/2020-11-15/bougainville-conman-king-still-on-the-run-independence-png/12879932.

Then onward, up the road still as smooth as chiffon, to Panguna. I'd heard and read so much about this place, knew how long it had been abandoned, but I wasn't prepared for the sheer magnitude of its scale and desolation: roofless cathedrals of metal that once housed ball mills, compactors that made the copper into a liquid concentrate, towering conveyor belts, giant slabs of concrete on which there had once been mess halls for hundreds of staff at a time. The whole ensemble reminded me of the abandoned mining colony in the movie *Aliens*. The complex went on for miles in every direction, a scurry of feeder roads, lanes and abandoned buildings. Much of the metal had been taken already, sold on for scrap.

We drove through the ghost slopes of the once mountain of Panguna and into the pit itself, with its phosphorescent and polluted pools of water – the purple, blue, azure and green colours on display the result of chemical coagulation – and rocks discoloured into kaleidoscopes of green and dark blue by the copper. From the lips of the mine to its base, the drive took 15 minutes. Back in the day this was a 24-hour operation of noise, heat and light, as three shift crews worked in diggers to excavate the soil and load it into the giant compressors for sorting. Not now. The mine was silent. But it was still active. Indented all around the pit site were brown tarpaulins held up with wooden poles. Close to each of these tents were three or four people hacking at the rock. Old men, middle-aged men, young men, and boys who looked as young as 10 were attacking the rock and soil with shovels and trowels; some were using their hands. They bundled up the rock onto their stomachs and then cradled it onto a griddle where one of the team would wash the soil off in the hope of finding trace elements of gold, or even a chunk. We talked to one of the teams – a man called James, two of his sons and their cousin – who said they'd been working on their patch of slope for more than two years. Each man was bare-chested, sweat rivulets dripping from their shoulders and chests.

And it was deeply hazardous work they were engaged in. Apart from frequent landslides, the risks that came from sticking hands deep into toxic soil on a regular basis were immense. The men and children worked with mercury for separation of the gold from the rock. Working incorrectly with that element could lead to mental illness, death or serious injury. This is what is quaintly termed 'artisanal mining'.[6]

6   Ciaran O'Faircheallaigh et al., 'Small-Scale Mining in Bougainville: Impacts and Policy Responses: Interim Report on Research Findings', Griffith University and State, Society and Governance in Melanesia, dpa.bellschool.anu.edu.au/sites/default/files/publications/attachments/2016-07/interim researchfindings_ssm_bougainville_260516.pdf.

It was a world away from the technological and mechanical implements used on Panguna in the 1970s and 1980s. The fossickers stayed for weeks at a time up at the Panguna site, mauling, grabbing and scrabbling at the rock, then headed into Arawa to the small hideaway stores that weighed, assayed and paid them in cash for their wares. It could be lucrative. Gold worth more than A$40 million leaves Bougainville each year, a tiny amount compared to what it would be onsold for, a tiny amount compared to the billions' worth of gold still in the ground. More than 10,000 Bougainvilleans engage in this work.[7]

We asked James how much he was making. He didn't volunteer a direct answer but said he was able to pay for school fees for his younger children and other relatives back in the village; his comment triggered a memory of an evocatively titled academic article – a rare thing in itself – that I had read some time earlier. The article was entitled 'Paying a School Fee Is a Father's Duty'.[8] James didn't look affluent, and if earnings were truly equated with hard labour, he certainly had more than earned his share; I didn't begrudge him one cent. I peeked inside his family's tent on the way back to the car. There were two bits of shipping pallet for the miners to sleep on, a couple of rusty pots and pans, two cups, an exercise book with a picture of a bird of paradise on the front, and a candle bearing the image of Our Lady of Fatima. Immediately outside the flaps of the tent, a small pyramid of sweet potatoes was stacked, with a fresh-looking Bougainville flag on top.

On the way back home, Eddie and I talked about whether the mine would ever reopen in the manner in which it had once operated. Bougainville Copper still exists as a company; Rio Tinto divested itself of its shares in 2016, and the governments in Buka and Port Moresby are each 36.4-per cent shareholders, but progress towards reopening the mine has stalled, although there has been no shortage of companies angling for the chance to start it up. It has been shut for more than 30 years now. However, that estimated A$60 billion of minerals sitting under the soil represents the best chance Bougainville has of being able to fund its independence.[9]

---

7   Anthony Regan, Ciaran O'Faircheallaigh and Tony Corbett, 'Artisanal and Small-Scale Mining (ASM) in Bougainville: Raising Government Revenue', PowerPoint presentation delivered at the Bougainville Revenue and Tax Summit, 27–29 September 2017, Buka, Autonomous Region of Bougainville, www.abg.gov.pg/images/misc/14._Taxing_Artisal_Small_Scale_Mining_in_B-ville_ (Regan).pdf.

8   Karen Sykes, 'Paying a School Fee is a Father's Duty: Critical Citizenship in Central New Ireland', *American Ethnologist* 28, no. 1 (2001), 5–31, jstor.org/stable/3095114.

9   For an analysis of Bougainville's progress on fiscal autonomy, see Chand, *Fiscal Autonomy*.

It would be costly and risky to reopen. Not counting the expense of the environmental clean-up, there would also be the costs of replacing equipment, ensuring the site is safe, refurbishing transport corridors and hiring staff, including the consultants, advisers, engineers, lawyers and others who don't actually work the mines but are essential to its well-oiled wheels. And then, the laws. Bougainville's mining laws are in place already – they constitute one of the powers that have been drawn down[10] – but many others would be needed, too, to cover everything from work visas to environmental remediation, and to ensure that adherence to these laws did not languish in the magical jungle of paper tigers, enforced by a team of effective bureaucrats. A fully operational mine, along with its seed money for independence, still seems a far-off prospect. There has been progress on this, at least. In 2022, the Bougainville government and landowners from the Panguna mine area reached a joint resolution to reopen the Panguna copper and gold mine. It is the first step on a long road, but an important one.

10   McKenna, 'Status and Implementation', 10.

9

Buka's bestseller

Of all the books nestled in the Unity library, the one most sought after was nearly a century old, written by a woman whose once house in Walton Street, Oxford, I would have walked by for many years without knowing that our paths would one day cross on this distant shore.

Her name was Beatrice Blackwood, and her book was proving so popular in the library that two copies had already been stolen, and the remaining copy was marked with a sticker carrying the note 'Library use only'. It was for sale elsewhere in Buka. The Adventist religious bookshop was selling copies for 200 kina (A$80) and, cost notwithstanding, there were ample customers. A local impresario scanned an out-of-focus copy of the book and was selling flash drives with their contents for a discount.

The book consisted of 600 pages of small-font, dry scholarly text and was entitled *Both Sides of Buka Passage*.[1] First published in 1934, it had been long out of print until a publishing press in Port Moresby reissued a gorgeous, illustrated version early in the last decade. There were 80 glossy photoplates, along with maps and drawings, including pictures of the spirits of the dead drawn on the inside covers. The book offered a literary portal into the past and evoked a time when all of PNG was something of an anthropologist's playground.

Anthropology is the study of human societies and their development. The academic vogue of what was a relatively new discipline in the 1930s originated in a desire to find a place as different from one's own as

---

1   Beatrice Blackwood, *Both Sides of Buka Passage: An Ethnographic Study of Social, Sexual, and Economic Questions in the North-Western Solomon Islands* (Oxford: Clarendon Press, 1934).

possible, hoping that a fellow researcher hadn't planted their gumboots there already, and write a long book about the cradle-to-grave goings-on there.

The 'empty' maps of PNG were regarded as the ideal location to pursue such endeavours. As well as Blackwood, there was the Pole, Bronislaw Malinowski[2] in the Trobriand Islands, and Margaret Mead,[3] an American who conducted her research on Manus Island. The anthropologists worked alone, enmeshed in timeless academic tangles of petty jealousy, insecurity and competition over the status of their respective publishing presses.

The level of detail they sought was extraordinary. At the archives in Oxford one damp, early autumn morning, I found a 28-page guide that Beatrice took with her to Bougainville entitled *Plan of Fieldwork*,[4] a detailed paint-by-numbers handbook on what to look for. Among the information to be acquired were: tribal relations; clans and subclans; personal appearance and domestic arrangements; cleanliness of teeth; types of games played and magic conducted; ceremonies; mythology; decorative art; vegetation, fauna and mineralogical properties of the soil; and the lyrics of lullabies the people sang. Skulls were to be measured, rainfall recorded daily and the temperature gauged thrice a day. The anthropologist was expected to appraise the extent to which the language enabled fine distinctions and nuances, although how such judgements and determinations were to be made by someone who didn't know any of the patois prior to arrival was anyone's guess.

The major focus in the guide was on sex, to such an extent that it would have made a satyr blush. The anthropologist was asked to record details of 'caressing, sexual acts, songs … [the] character of love and love-mating … [and] brother and sister in sex'. Also, to be recorded: conception, childbirth, child-rearing, initiation ceremonies, the everyday experience of marriage.

2   Bronislaw Malinowski, *Argonauts of the Western Pacific: An Account of Native Enterprise and Adventure in the Archipelagos of Melanesian New Guinea* (London: Routledge, 1979).
3   Margaret Mead, *Growing Up in New Guinea: A Study of Adolescence and Sex in Primitive Societies* (Melbourne: Penguin Books, 1942).
4   All uncited citations below come from material contained in the 'Blackwood Papers', Pitt Rivers Museum, prm.ox.ac.uk/blackwood-papers.

I was fascinated by this book and bought a copy, but it took weeks of assiduous effort to finish it. The authorial voice is humourless, stern, schoolmarmish. Beatrice reminded me of the hockey captain in an English boarding-school novel, the sort of person who would take relish in tape-measuring a fresh corpse. She followed the fieldwork guide exactingly, and her writing style was, to be charitable, dutiful. I could understand why people liked the pictures, the photos and the now sepia quality of the text, but its narrative was not gripping by any means. An academic contemporary of hers acclaimed it as 'compact, well organised and straight to point', which, even by the criteria of the ivory tower, was a judgement that bended the *actualité*. I didn't particularly want to spend any longer with the author than the time necessary to trudge through to the end of her tome.

Then I found her letters and diaries that day in Oxford, and I began to like her more and more. The woman of the letters is knowing, amusing, ironic, wry and perplexed. She uses shorthand such as 'dope' for information and is an expert in the zinging aside. She is amusingly disparaging about the colonial set she comes across, who, to a person, seem to be gossipy drunks with unfounded airs and graces. Her accounts of the epic feats of drinking and complex personality-based machinations within the white set are scabrous, hilarious and touching. The doctor she meets 'is a pig-headed, ignorant individual with no more idea about what the natives [sic] are like than the man on the moon'. Mrs Haddon and her husband, who own a plantation growing coconuts on the other side of the mission, 'are said to be very nice when sober', but one gains the impression that such abstemiousness was fleeting. The only people not getting sozzled are the missionaries, 'and they are duller than ditch water'. Beatrice is propositioned by a couple of chiefs and meets a woman whose father was eaten in a cannibal rite. She is given a possum-tooth necklace and asks: 'Shall I wear it at the next college ball?' Most of all, she is candid about herself, about the challenges she faced and the insecurities she fought on a daily basis.

The letters and diaries have the makings of a book of picaresque journalling from the South Seas. Arthur Thomson, her supervisor and the man to whom she wrote the letters, thought they were worthy of publication. Her wary answer ensured they wouldn't be. 'Of course, edit them carefully and please do not leave in any of my remarks about the missionaries [and] planters, because although I heartily disapprove of both species, they both have been kind to me, and I must consider very carefully anything I say in print because it will get back here eventually'. She embodied the enduring bind of the academic, wanting to be read but feeling unable to write in a manner that would make one likely to be read beyond the narrowest of constituencies.

It is a continuing problem of representation, especially since most researchers who write about PNG continue to be not from that country. The issue remains now as it does then, namely, how can foreign (white) researchers be trusted to represent Melanesian subjects? Most of the people publishing about PNG today are academics, a small band who either know each other, or know of each other, about as well as residents of an isolated village cut off from the world by high valleys. As in any community, there are friendships, feuds, romances, quarrels over money, and places in the pecking order. I once worked at a research institution dedicated to researching Melanesia, which, when funding was cut, descended into factions and divisions as opaque and personality-based as the decisions of the governments they sought to explain through their research reports.

I've lodged in this academic village myself over the years, and many of the people who remain there are my friends. I was always happy to see them if we overlapped in the Holiday Inn or bumped into each other on the Monday morning flights up from Australia. Yet, here too, there would often be a difference between what was said with abandon at the Gekko Bar and what was reported in an academic paper. In person, many academics are the most chatty, gossipy, interesting people one is likely to meet; yet on the page, some can be leaden. Dogmatic conventions of academic writing prevent many from writing the way they talk. This leads many an academic author to feel duty-bound to inflict on their readers arrow after arrow of tortured and bloodless sentences, thereby consigning their painstakingly curated and passionately analysed knowledge to small print runs read by few beyond their scholarly acolytes, with at least half of whom they are likely to be feuding. Some academic writing conventions cloak everything in reference to an abstruse theoretical framework, with a prose style hostile to the vivid term. 'I am not a travel writer, I am a serious researcher,' harrumphs one of the Australians in Bougainvillean author Regis Tove Stella's *Mata Sara* (*Crooked Eyes*).[5] This is a genre in which devotees claw out the word 'hubbub' from a draft and nail the word

---

5   Regis Tove Stella, *Mata Sara (Crooked Eyes)* (Port Moresby: University of Papua New Guinea Press, 2010), 9.

'discontent' in its stead. I have dipped in and out of academia because I find the occlusions of scholarly writing more of a chore than I am prepared to put up with.

At least these academic works are published, if rarely read. Some of the anaesthetised bureaucratic form I was engaging in during my time in Bougainville did not lead to publication. I'd taken to helping shoulder some of the program's reporting burden. Compared to academia, even more of the good stuff was deemed to require excision: sensitive internal politics, accounts of foibles, zesty antics and maddening episodes – the real explanatory marrow that accounted for why the mosaic was the way it was. Instead, it was all reporting on 'capacity development plans', 'frameworks' and the like. It meant that what was presented on the page felt incomplete and inadequate. I recalled a conversation I had once in West Africa with the gender adviser to a higher-up in the United Nations. 'I know he's not reading my reports,' she said to me. I was sure she was right, but how did she know? 'Because I put the c-word in on the second page of most of them and he never pulls me up about it,' she replied. We put a lot of work into our reports, but sometimes I felt I could have buried the translation of the Rosetta Stone in some of them and no-one would have found it. One of my favourite mordant statistics is that, of all the reports available on the World Bank website, close to a third of them have never been opened, not even once.[6]

Maybe it was the long nights in Buka, maybe it was our shared connection with Oxford, but I began to feel, to use an anthropologist's term, a kinship with Beatrice. She was engaged in the same wrestle of what to present, and how to present it, in the same place as I was. Now that I knew her beyond her academic writing, I found her a source of solace, fascination, guidance and company. I was determined to go seek out her ghost.

6   Doerte Doemeland and James Trevino, 'Which World Bank Reports Are Widely Read?', The World Bank Development Economics Vice Presidency Operations and Strategy Unit Policy Research Working Paper 6851, documents1.worldbank.org/curated/en/387501468322733597/pdf/WPS6851.pdf.

10

Beatrice's Bougainville

When Beatrice Blackwood sailed from Australia to the mandated territory of New Guinea on the *S.S. Montoro* in 1929, she had just turned 40, held a position as an anthropologist from Oxford University, had previously completed fieldwork among native Americans in the state of Arizona, and was closing in on her research goal of finding 'an island somewhere in the Pacific with the least possible amount of contact with white people and go and live in it'. Funded by the unambiguously named Committee for Research on the Problems of Sex, her plan was to discern the goings-on in a 'primitive' society, for such was the endeavour in vogue in anthropology at the time.

Her journey took her from England around the Cape of Good Hope, across the Indian Ocean, through the Southern Ocean to Sydney, then onward to Rabaul, the capital of the Territory of New Guinea. This final leg was 'chock-full of missionaries', she wrote to her supervisor, Thomson, in her first dispatch, which she penned on the Scottish thistle letterhead of the shipping company. She shared a cabin with an old island hand, a woman returning with her newborn child. In the manner of expatriates to this day, the woman was only too happy to wax knowledgeably to the newcomer about her wide breadth of understanding in such a manner as to make the tenderfoot feel apprehensive. Upon arrival in Rabaul, Beatrice spent a week in a hotel she described as being an 'abomination of desolation'. She shared a room with a woman who was the chief suspect in a murder investigation following her husband's death from arsenic poisoning three months earlier.

Beatrice met with Chinnery, the government anthropologist, who was facilitating her entry into what she hoped would be an impenetrable fastness. Bougainville seemed like a ready-made sort of place to fulfil Beatrice's objective of splendid isolation. Large parts were untouched by either the governmental or missionary contact that anthropologists so dreaded, as either presence was deemed to sully their pursuit of the authentically exotic. The Australians notionally controlled the territory, having taken over from Germany as part of the settlement of Versailles.

Chinnery gave her a revolver to protect herself on location but, when she arrived, she found that the major danger she faced was tedium. The site selected for her did not match her expectations. That was the island of Petats, just off Buka Island. She found the people there were what she called 'erstwhile savages', living in not quite as primitive and primordial a state as she had been hoping to find. The people were at the 'half-sophisticated-half-barbarian stage, where one doesn't know which way to treat them, and they are overrun by missionaries', she lamented. There had been way too much preaching and choral music, and it 'was distinctly disconcerting to find the blighters going to church every evening and twice on a Sunday'. Anthropologists at that time were congenitally contemptuous about missionaries, my theory being that this was partially out of an insecurity that they would find the missionaries to be more embedded, well-informed and linguistically adroit than were the anthropologists themselves.[1]

As my anthropologist friend Siobhan surmised, there might have been sexism in the choice of location: the men of the Australian colonial administration did not feel that 'off-the-map' areas were places for women. Another location, Kurtatchi, seemed to offer richer pickings. It was on the larger Bougainville Island and closer to the image of authentic primordialism that had been in her mind's eye ever since Oxford. In her book, she renders her arrival in Kurtatchi as positively natural and matter-of-fact. Punari, the village's headman and paramount chief for the area, invited her for a visit. She liked what she saw and paid for a house elevated on stilts to be built for her in the centre of the village, which enabled her to watch the comings and goings as if she were atop a panopticon. Beatrice brought along to Kurtatchi a servant called Ross, 'who had

---

1   The first Christian mission had been established not that long before Blackwood arrived in the Buka area. The mission had been set up in Kieta – a long way from Buka and Petats – in 1901. In Buka, the first mission station began only in 1910, so contact was relatively recent.

worked for white people and knew what was required of him'. (Ross was named after the white man his father had once worked for.) She told the residents of Kurtatchi that her people – who lived very far away – had sent her there to see what kind of folk they were. The reason she needed to ask them so many detailed questions was to help her give a full and well-rounded account back to her own chief. 'The natives are unspoiled and unsophisticated … [I]nstead of thinking that they are doing me a favour in talking to me, they are proud to have me and very keen to tell me,' she wrote to Thomson. The backstory is that Mrs Haddon, daughter of Parkinson, the Dane, had helped to facilitate the visit.

Regardless of how she got there, Beatrice was a woman of clearly remarkable gifts of persuasion. She was able to persuade the residents of Kurtatchi to cough up no end of details about their customs, secrets and taboos. She persuaded young men to draw pictures of the *urar*, the spirits of the dead, and acquired from them bull roarers – wooden, spatula-like contraptions that, when swung fast on a rope, made an ominous rumble. Young men would come up to her, unbidden, with bunches of mulched leaves and whisper how they could be used to gain the favours of women, information exchanged for a few of Beatrice's cigarette butts and bandages to heal their suppurating tropical leg ulcers. Young women invited her to their menstruation ceremonies, and she was present at a few births. She asked and was duly told in elaborate detail about tightly held poisoning techniques. Beatrice took photographs of the women and men who had undergone cicastration, an ornate process of body tattooing by which marks were made on the skin with flints of glass and coral, but she told Thomson that her interest in participant research didn't extend that far. She ripped pages from her notebooks and asked the villagers – most of whom would have been holding a pencil or crayon for the first time – to draw pictures of the spirits of the dead. She collected details of the people's diet with a view to ascertaining its vitamin content; recorded temperatures and rainfall every morning, noon and evening; and carried out body measurements. Initially, she defecated behind a bush but changed her toileting habits when the villagers found such actions prudish; feeling no necessity to maintain English decorum, she subsequently dropped her trousers to relieve herself as and when.

Evenings were a fertile time for gathering stories. The villagers were 'afraid to walk in the bush after dark, as there are devils in there', so they crowded around her house and told her stories. She gave old copies of the English Sunday broadsheet *The Observer* to the men of the village, who used them to roll up their tobacco as they talked. Blackwood collected 91 verbatim reports of the villagers' actual dreams, told to her in the early light of morning when she'd wander around the village asking 'if anyone had any dreams the previous night'. She happily pried into every villager's sex life and penned accounts of her interviews entitled 'The homosexual maniac', 'The man who didn't know about sex', 'The man who copulated with a dog', 'The woman caught with a lover', 'The impotent man named Wasein', 'The unfaithful wife returns and a man is killed' and 'The woman who had sex with a banana'. Extraordinary stuff: I couldn't imagine asking any person in Bougainville such questions about the inner recesses of their interior lives, lest they throw me headfirst into the fast-moving current of the Buka Passage. And what reception would a South Sea Islander be given if they showed up in an Oxford college putting forward inquisition as a methodology?

Beatrice travelled extensively in her year in Bougainville, with a haversack on one shoulder and her tabby cat, Felicia, often on the other, and a long line of what she called the natives behind her carrying her bed, table, chair, typewriter, pots and pans, food boxes and a bathtub that would be used for collecting rainwater for drinking. When the people of Kurtatchi would travel to other villages for ceremonies, she arrived in tow with the men, brandishing a spear and blowing on a conch shell as the occasion demanded. She went hunting with the men for possums in the forest. Some of her stories reminded me of Indiana Jones, the 1980s movie character modelled on the academics of Beatrice's time, who boldly went into parts unknown looking for fortune and glory.[2]

In return for stories, dreams and items, Beatrice traded sticks of tobacco, loin cloths, calico and metal bolts bought from the Chinese trade stores in Buka Town. Along with her fieldwork diaries, accounts, maps, drawings and pictures, she packed over 400 items in her seachests and lugged them back to the Pitt Rivers Museum in Oxford. The haul included shells, pottery, spoons, a spatula, a leaf, fishhooks, stones carved to look like fish, panpipes, over 40 specimens of human hair, paddles carved with human faces, a canoe, the three bull roarers, and a wooden musical instrument registered in the collection as a Jew's harp, a term that has happily gone out of circulation in the years since. She sneaked back two deformed skulls

---

2   Steven Spielberg, dir., *Indiana Jones and the Temple of Doom* (Los Angeles: Paramount Pictures, 1984); referencing Indiana Jones's iconic, tongue-in-cheek saying: 'Fortune and glory, kid. Fortune and glory.'

and resisted the urge to dig up any more, lest the missionaries catch wind of what she was doing. These and other items were given to the Pitt Rivers Museum, where she worked as curator from her return in 1931 until her death 44 years later. In the spirit of devotion to her research, Beatrice would don some of her collection for the annual college ball.

In my visit to the museum, I found a few of her gathered items out on display and the rest available to view upon request, with the exception of the skulls, their current location being unknown. In a well-lit room around the back, a curator laid out for me many of the other artefacts from storage onto sheets of sheeny white paper. The items looked as fresh as if Beatrice had just deposited them. I donned white woollen gloves that made me feel like a snooker referee and was particularly fascinated to see the two *upe* that she had brought back. The *upe* formed the centrepiece of three initiation ceremonies from which a boy becomes a man and looks, she wrote, like the headwear of the *urar*, the spirits of the dead. It was a hat of tightly wound straw that the boy's hair would grow into, to a point where the hair reached such a length the *upe* could fit snugly on his head. Blackwood was the first to write about these shrouded ceremonies in her book. In her diaries, she wrote how some boys, each sporting an *upe,* would sit under her verandah at night and scramble for a few drags on the cigarette butts she flicked out of the house.

As already noted, the *upe* is now the central symbol on the cobalt flag of Bougainville, and although the ceremonies were still taking place, I'd never seen the hat before in real life. They are remarkable constructions. Each was about a foot in length, the colour of straw with ochre-coloured block patterns. I traced my fingers on its grooves and folds, felt the nobbled texture of the straw and wondered at the amount of time it would take to fill in the insides. My hair grows quickly, but even Samson would have been challenged to grow tresses that reached this deeply inside. Having to balance the *upe* in such circumstances without it falling off would have constantly been an immense challenge.

An elderly woman was in the exhibit room with me. She was working as a volunteer cataloguing exhibits and testing the patience of the staff by continuously asking them elementary questions about how to use Microsoft Excel. The woman remembered Beatrice near the end of her life. I vainly hoped to elicit some sort of searing 'across the generations' insight, but all the woman could remember was that the old anthropologist liked drinking strong tea. Such are the challenges entailed in chasing ghosts, but they also reflected for me the ephemerality of all our work. It was Bougainville to which now fell the responsibility for keeping her memory aflicker.

I loved the unvarnished Beatrice of the diaries, where the self-assured woman of the book reveals herself to be beset with the foibles of academics from time immemorial. Insecurity and self-doubt gnaw constantly. She wonders about the utility of all the cases of material she was collecting. She wakes up with panic attacks about how she is ever going to write a book about a society she doesn't understand. She wonders frequently what the point of it all is and if anyone will read her book. 'I hope my days or most of it [sic] are spent in the acquisition of knowledge, but I don't know that we are any better off when we've acquired it,' she writes, close to the end of her year in the then territory.

You can almost hear the self-doubt rattling like hot water coursing through an old pipe in wintertime. She compares herself unfavourably to her fellow anthropologists and wallows in their perceived slights. She worries in particular that her words aren't ever going to strike the literary high notes of Malinowski. She grouses about having to collect a medley of objects and totems to keep on the good side of her superiors at Oxford. I empathised entirely with her complaints of getting bored with material while knowing that much more polishing of it was required before it could be published. She reveals how she feels isolated and often deeply lonely. She longs for the theatre, newspapers and Sunday drives to English pubs. Her only friend is Felicia the tabby cat.

Beatrice deliberately took herself into the far-beyond to find people as different from herself as possible, then felt thoroughly lonely, as she had nothing in common with them. Haven't many of us felt an insatiable curiosity to travel away from our home and its mundane familiarity to discover the new, only to recoil with surprise at the unbidden discovery that the distance we put between those we left behind and ourselves provides not solace but deeper awareness of why our connectedness matters?

If we had met in a bar in PNG, I'm sure we would have had a wonderful time, swapping absurdities until the trellis was rattled for last call. I'm sure we would have had a great time rolling our eyes about the pomposity of government and some of the people who constitute it. She was scathing about the way the colonial officials gilded their progress reports to the League of Nations in a manner not l dissimilar to the contortions I and others of my ilk were performing in our reports. Even her descriptions of people feel similar. The C-grade-quality district officer she meets – 'He is a self-important individual who feels it incumbent upon himself to exercise his authority on every possible occasion' – reminded me of one boss in Buka whose intellectual comfort levels didn't extend far beyond beaky perusal of the monthly timesheet and mumbling into his moustache about the importance of adhering to unspecified 'protocols' that supposedly governed our interactions with Simon and his colleagues.

Despite all this, I imagine that this night in the bar would have ended with us both in a woebegone state. The letters and diary entries for Beatrice's last months are sad. She exhibits clear signs of melancholic staleness. The droll humour that previously characterises her letters has ebbed away. By this point, Punari appears to be in a huff – she indicates in her letters that he had been cuckolded by another. That would explain her sour mood and may well be the case, but I also wondered if he'd slunk off because he had grown tired of continually answering her probing questions. By the end of her time there, it is clear she is ready to leave. There is not one reference to her feelings upon departure in either her diaries or her field journals, or to the ultimate fate of Felicia the tabby cat. In one entry, she is collecting rainwater measures, and in the next she is on a clipper bound for North America, sharing time on deck with a troupe of professional wrestlers before voyaging on, back to Oxford. Writing the book left her flat, but it was positively reviewed in all the right journals, the status of words from peers more important than a royalty cheque. Much of what she expresses in her letters – the self-doubt, her questioning the worth of her endeavour – resonates with many of us who feel the tension between the pull to pursue a passion we care about deeply, and the pushback from a world more inclined to celebrating banality.

The more I read of Beatrice, the more curious I became to see Kurtatchi for myself, the place where this stranger wandered unannounced and mapped the most intimate details of peoples' lives. It was a place still so seemingly off the map that it still didn't feature in either contemporary charts or Google Maps. Part of this was academic curiosity. In the years that followed, Beatrice Blackwood's work was held up as the baseline against which all researchers assessed change in Bougainville. In that spirit, I wanted to see how much the place had changed in the years since the first publication of *Both Sides of Buka Passage*, years that had seen the Second World War; the arrival of a large-scale mining operation and, with it, an influx into Bougainville of people from elsewhere in PNG and abroad; the end of the Australian colonial administration; two unilateral and almost completely unacknowledged declarations of Bougainville independence; an always uneasy relationship within PNG; a 10-year conflict; and now, 15 or so years of this cheerless peace. The other reason I wanted to see Kurtatchi was that I was bored of simply hanging around in my house reading books and going for the occasional run and hamstring-testing bushwalk through the hilled forests of Buka Island on the weekends.

'You ever been to Kurtatchi?' I asked Eddie one day. 'Kurtatchi? I've passed by,' he said, 'but no problem getting there. It'll be easy to arrange.' It was not, and in that dwells a tale of modern Bougainville.

11

Plan A

I knew it would not just be a matter of hopping on one of the taxi boats over the passage, hiring a car and us driving there for a look-see, but the way it all unfolded still surprised me.

In Bougainville, as elsewhere in PNG, much land is 'customary', which among other things means one has to be invited by someone connected to the land-owning clan. If I had walked around Eddie's village or surrounds without his permission, I would have suffered the fate of a colleague who had parked there for a walk, only to come back and find all his tyres slashed. Visitors were required to seek permission and follow customary rituals.

Kurtatchi was located outside of Eddie's geographical area, and our trip would require the blessing and assistance of The Honourable Joseph Watawi. He was the member of Bougainville's House of Representatives for the local constituency and lived in the sprawling township of Kokopau on the other side of the passage, where once the land had belonged to Mrs Haddon. I had run into Joseph every now and again over the years and liked him a great deal. A former mineworker and trade unionist, he was the first vice-president in the first autonomous government and, subsequently, minister for consumer affairs. At the time, he gloried in being one of two members of the unofficial opposition in Bougainville's parliament. I liked Joseph's slightly quaint, olde-worlde English expressions, such as 'Holy Moses', 'stir the pot' and 'we are cooking something in the kitchen', and his ever-present sense of puckishness. He was gregarious, pugnacious, bombastic, funny, avuncular, smart and a gadfly of the highest order. When we went to pay him homage at his house overlooking Buka Passage, he was wearing a pair of rugby league shorts and a 'Bougainville – land of the blacks' T-shirt, and he was cultivating a greying beard that made him look like gangsta rapper Ice Cube.

Another characteristic of Joseph was his sense of curiosity about the world and openness to the notion that something could be learned from finding out what was happening beyond his own islands' shores. It was one of the many curiosities about Bougainville: the political class fervently desired political independence, but there was limited engagement with the outside world that could grant it. When a delegation of French naval officers arrived from their territories in the Pacific in 2018 to commemorate the arrival of Louis de Bougainville, for example, it seemed a perfect opportunity to lobby, but only a handful of politicians showed up.

Joseph had travelled a few years before to my homeland, Northern Ireland, on a delegation to look at referendums, and his abiding memory seemed to be of the bitterness he found there. 'Holy Moses,' he would say to me often when we'd bump into each other, as if hearing my accent triggered in him a Pavlovian response. 'There is no forgiveness. I was amazed. You guys really still hate each other so very much. You need to arrange some reconciliation ceremonies between each other.' He and Eddie were old pals from Arawa but on different sides from conflict times, Eddie with the Bougainville Revolutionary Army and Joseph working as part of the national government's various interim authorities. Both were fervently pro-independence. Political differences back then didn't stop them now, however. Joseph had recently bought Eddie a bicycle for him to travel the 20 kilometres from his home into town, but its wheels quickly revealed themselves no match for the atrocious state of the roads.

Joseph was as confident as Eddie that arranging a visit to Kurtatchi would be a doddle. He was happy to help on the condition that I'd ferry him up some Jameson Irish Whiskey from duty-free the next time I came up from Australia. He suggested a two-step strategy: a short trip down now to introduce ourselves and our objectives, and then a longer visit a few weeks afterwards, whiskey in tow. On the drive down for the first visit, we passed a thick but unremarkable stand of trees. This, Joseph said, was one of the places where young boys would live in complete seclusion for up to three months at the beginning of their *upe* initiation. These long and involved ceremonies continued to take up most of the boys' teenage years, as did puberty rituals for teenage girls. With obvious allegory, a part of the ceremony for the girls was structured around shimmying up a banana tree and throwing the fruit down.

A few minutes further down the road we arrived in Kurtatchi, which seemed smaller than I had imagined it from Beatrice's descriptions. It consisted of about 20 houses painted lime-green, built by the side of the road. The most prominent feature of the village was a giant white cross; the Christians must have got here too, after Beatrice. We found a man with a wizened faced sitting by the roadside waiting for a bus. Joseph divined serendipity – we had happened upon the village chief, a successor to the Punari of Beatrice's time. The chief was in his late forties – much younger than I would have placed him. On his T-shirt was a Japanese manga character firing a thunderbolt from his index finger. Staying a safe distance from us were a few people looking bewildered at the sight of us clambering out of a car unannounced. I could see them all backing ever so slowly away from us, much as I back away whenever I see someone with a charity clipboard heading towards me.

The chief nodded his head vigorously when we mentioned Beatrice's name. Whether this was because he had heard of her previously, her ghost was exerting a continued presence in the village or he thought this was the correct or polite thing to do (given our unexpected arrival, yammering about a long-dead, white-skinned woman) was an open question. We told him about the 400 objects Beatrice had traded for and their location in the Pitt Rivers Museum in Oxford. He looked surprised that a village such as his would ever have produced such a trove. He was even more astounded when I told him that some of these items were being gawped at by thousands of visitors each day. Kurtatchi looked today like a place with no statues. A contemporary anthropologist would find fewer initiations to record, no artefacts to take away but, from the look of the chief's arms, definitely still some cicastrated people to take pictures of.

The village was built on the bones of the old one; Kurtatchi had been abandoned during the Crisis, and its people had moved back only a few years prior to our visit. The chief said he'd call a meeting the following day to let everyone know and confirmed that we were welcome to return a few weeks later. Joseph suggested we buy a pig and bring it down with us to show our bona fides. We would roast the pig in tribute to the spirit of Beatrice Blackwood, former headman Punari and the people of Kurtatchi from yesteryear and today. This was a strategy Beatrice would have heartily endorsed; she paid regularly for ceremonies in Kurtatchi so that she could write about them in her field notes. The whiskey I brought from duty-free would lubricate the event even further. Indeed, out of prudence, it might be a good idea to bring an extra bottle just in case, proposed Joseph. It all sounded good and novel to me. Two bottles of whiskey it would be. I'd also buy the chief a copy of Beatrice's book.

In the weeks following our initial sortie, I gave Eddie five 100-kina notes for the pig, which he bought in his village. He trussed it with rope, threw it in the back of a truck, then wrangled it onto a banana boat for the quick trip over the Buka Passage. Some of Joseph's 'staff officers' – another one of those wonderful olde-worlde English phrases that punctuated so much of Papua New Guinean English – put the pig in a car and drove it down to Kurtatchi. Everything seemed to be in order, and I woke up on the morning of the feast with a set of paragraph headings in my mind: type of food served, how many people, ghost memories of Beatrice, picaresque touches. I checked my phone to find a message from Joseph. 'Get over here now,' it read. 'We are having a major problem.'

12

Plan B and whiskey to the rescue

I found Joseph and Eddie sitting on two wobbly, once-white plastic chairs in the 'Salty Eyes', the parliamentarians' house-cum-second-hand emporium that overlooked the Buka Passage. A Crystal Palace–Liverpool football game was playing in the background on a small television, and a few children were sitting around eating plates of cold rice and bully beef.

Joseph was looking stressed, lamenting his inability to get to somewhere in his very own constituency as compared to this Englishwoman from close to a century before. 'What magic did this Beatrice Blackwood have that enabled her to come to the village of Kurtatchi and ingratiate herself so easily with the people?' he asked. 'How was she able to do this in 1929, when we are having such difficulties doing the same now? We made the initial visit. We properly arranged this visit. And it has completely gone to shit. My boys were nearly attacked when they went there this morning to try to get our pig back. Fucking fuck.'

What had happened the evening before in Kurtatchi was a case study in how little can be predictably planned in the Autonomous Region of Bougainville. It sounded like it had been quite the night. Grouching, jealousy, suspicions, finger-pointing, shoving and conspiracy theories about our visit had erupted at the meeting and were spinning wildly in all sorts of directions. How much money was this white man paying Joseph? Just what was our real agenda? What did we want to take away? How many riches were we going to be making from writing a book about Kurtatchi?

If only they knew about the gruel-like margins of the publishing industry, I groaned, and marvelled all the more at the way Beatrice had managed to sally in so easily by contrast. The people in the village had divided into two feuding groups: those who could see the trip for the curiosity that it was, and those who saw undertows of wider, malign intent and fundamentally distrusted the intentions of white foreigners. Joseph was embarrassed. I felt for him. He, too, was a chief, from the same clan line as Punari. He'd promised to take me, and now some villagers were putting up a roadblock – quite literally – on our plans.

It was now mid-morning. The pig that had gone to Kurtatchi the previous day had been returned and was looking a tad perplexed, tied up and slung across the driver's seat of a minibus outside Joseph's house. There it stayed for a few minutes before Joseph asked me if he could buy it off me at cost price, which I agreed to with alacrity, having already wondered what I was going to do with it otherwise. The hog was then promptly driven off to a reconciliation ceremony elsewhere; there were many of these ceremonies taking place leading up to the referendum, villagers divided during the Crisis making peace with each other before the vote. We poured some of the whiskey I'd brought along into what Joseph said were his best glasses, which he had recently purchased from the Chinese store. As soon as the liquid struck the base of the receptacles, they lit up like deranged disco lights. 'Neat, eh?' said Joseph. 'Had to pay extra to the China-man for them but it was well worth it.' I resolved to buy some for my kids, which I subsequently did, precipitating a detailed search of the items at Australian customs.

After two glasses of the strong stuff, we settled on a Plan B. We – I, Eddie, Joseph, his sons and two of his 'staff officers' – would go to check out other places in Beatrice's book, ones where our arrival would, hopefully, occasion less chance of inciting a wholesale village rumpus. Our rough itinerary would take two days to accomplish, with a night spent back in Buka in between. Our preparations were less thorough than those of Beatrice: in lieu of the bathtub, we took the remainder of the whiskey, 24 bottles of SP beer and two packets of cheese Twisties; then we hopped into Joseph's motorised banana boat (the MV *Salty Eyes*) and off we went. The other bottle of whiskey we left in reserve with Joseph's wife for the next day.

We followed the coast away from Kurtatchi, along the mangrove shoreline and towards the land that Beatrice had walked while on her way to record the details of the *upe* initiations. We docked at the edges of a plantation after 30 minutes of pleasure-cruising. Eddie and the officers clearing a narrow avenue through the grounds with his bush knife. The grounds were entirely overgrown, filled with lanky trees that no longer produced coconuts. Most of the plantations in Bougainville were in a similar state of disuse.

There were still some people around who looked as if they were long-term squatters. A man and woman came out of the bush with a jerry can to pour water on our feet: a tradition Beatrice recorded as being a means to wash away any untoward spirits that newcomers might bring. The couple and their two kids, who were hiding from us in trees just beyond the shoreline, were camped out there, fishing for *bêche-de-mer*, which they'd sell on to the Chinese stores in Buka. A few of these marine morsels were sitting in a blackened makeshift smoker, a saucepan with a tagine-like cover that reminded me of an *upe* in its dimensions. An example of French being a more romantic language than English, the literal translation of *bêche-de-mer* is 'slug of the sea'. In consistency, these little slugs looked like something between a chipolata sausage and a dog biscuit, but they were a windfall for the couple. *Bêche-de-mer* is a delicacy in China and Japan, and the couple would sell them to small, Chinese-run stores that operated behind high hoardings of corrugated metal, the next staging post in a long supply chain that would take the creatures all the way to restaurants throughout China and Japan. I asked the man if his kids were at school, and he answered in a roundabout way. He said he hoped the money would pay for them to attend next year. 'If I could get a shark fin, that would be really good,' he said. This was real economic development, cash put in a poor family's pocket and infinitely more useful than a 'policy tweak' or setting up a committee.

As we clambered back into the MV *Salty Eyes*, Joseph's son was wiping the inside of the boat with leaves he took from a plastic bag, to ensure the onward journey would be cleansed of any malevolent spirits picked up from the plantation. As we left, he threw the beer bottles into the water, and they bobbed away like apples.

The next morning, fresh bottle of whiskey uncorked, the same technical team went onward to the island of Petats, Beatrice's initial field site and among the places thought potentially to be one of the sites where Amelia

Earhart might have crashed on her round-the-world flight.[1] A film crew from National Geographic Channel had visited a few months earlier, Eddie helping the crew out as fixer, but no trace of the aviator had been found. On this morning, our arrival was ignored entirely. After a few hours there I understood why Beatrice couldn't wait to get away. It seemed a place remarkable primarily for how little was happening. We tramped upward to the field in the centre of the village where there was a school (its logo displaying two fat dolphins butting heads over a book) in the hope of finding someone to talk to, but there was nobody around. We heard the lilting sounds of a congregation singing: another place where the missionaries had done a thorough job. If this were a development project, the Church would have received top marks for sustainability.

'This is far too bloody quiet,' said Joseph. 'Let's go to Pororan.'

Pororan is the island farther up the coast and a place Beatrice described as home of particularly potent magic deployed for catching fish. She writes that on Pororan there were a couple of anointed men who sanded thick pebbles into the shape of a fish with impish little dots marked for eyes; they then chiselled leftward dents on the snout, which were always to point towards shore, and swaddled the fish with leaves for scales. The little fish would be thrown out into the sea; shoals of fish would swoosh towards them and into the fisherman's net.

Beatrice herself never made it to Pororan. She was waiting by the boat at dawn for the trip to begin only for none of the boatmen to show up. Her manservant Ross explained some weeks later what had happened: Beatrice had offered three sticks of tobacco for the trip, but the sailors got the hump, as they believed that the going rate was four sticks. Instead of saying there was a problem, they simply didn't show up, and I wondered as I read this whether there was a similar rationale underlying limited attendances in the offices of the Bougainville government. Nevertheless, somehow she managed to bring back two of the carved stone fish with her to Oxford. When I read her papers back in Oxford, I perched the two little fish either side of me as I worked. It was the first time they had been

---

1   'Is Amelia Earhart's Plane in the Waters of Bougainville?', *Pacific Waves*, Radio New Zealand, rnz.co.nz/international/programmes/datelinepacific/audio/2018691722/is-amelia-earhart-s-plane-in-the-waters-of-bougainville.

helped out of their storage boxes since she had deposited them upon her return all those years before. The little eyes on the fish reminded me of speckles on fairy bread.

Save for another giant white cross on the harbour and an unexpectedly strong 3G phone network, Pororan had the feel of a place little changed from what it would have been 90 years earlier. We walked around the island, a dander of about half an hour. There was no semblance of any government here. What Joseph and Eddie reckoned to be the majority of the population of the entire island were not on land but on the shoals, casting nets on sandbars or squatting in little wooden canoes just out to shore fishing for bonito, scooping and hooking them out of the water with a regular click of the rod. We waded into the waters to look at the boats, each of which had a little carved sigil on the front. Some depicted the beaks of eagles, others those of hornbills; they connoted respective clans of the region.

I felt a serenity about the place that I'm sure was due to knowing I was not going to have to stay too long here. I felt as far off the map as it was possible to be: Pororan was an hour's ride from any other island. The rain began to spit down from darkening shrouds of clouds, and Joseph signalled it was high time we got on our way. We bought a few of the fish and waded back onto our boat, me walking gingerly in the hope the plastic on my flip-flops would withstand the coral underneath, and everyone else walking out as nonchalantly as though treading on satin-lined pavement.

More wiping with leaves before departing, and, as the rain began to fall, we huddled together as if this action would keep us dry. I had a minor panic attack on the way, summoning fears in my mind of what would happen if I fell off this boat, and imagining how silently and completely I would sink into the sea. We had no life jackets. Joseph dozed off just as the squall intensified, grey rain lashing us from an acute angle and waves splashing onto the boat. Eddie put out his right hand and clicked his fingers back and forth in a slow rhythm. He was doing something that the Englishwoman had also written about. He was trying – and, as it turned out, failing utterly – to chase away the rain.

The journey continued in this character-building vein for hours, and I was happy to see the Tchibo Rock, which signalled we were close to Buka Town. This large outcrop in the passage looked like one could land a mini-helicopter on it. Beatrice recorded its story in her book. Tchibo was the name of a person who died when caught out by the fast-running waters of the passage and fell under the rock, his spirit carving the channels that break the reef and allow ships and boats to pass in and out. This was not the rock's first resting place, she'd written. The stories she recorded told that in each place Tchibo tried to move to, the *urar* chased it elsewhere. Beatrice had taken a picture of the rock, and no matter how many times I looked at it, it always seemed to be a different place in the present than it was during her time. Maybe it was my whiskey-goggles, but it seemed to be in a perceptibly different part of the passage that day.

Seeing Tchibo made me realise we were close, and I felt like kissing the rickety deck of the *Salty Eyes* upon arrival. When we got there, Joseph's wife had made fried rice. She began to cook the fish from Pororan. Joseph sent out for two more bottles of locally produced whiskey, a challenging tipple that smelled of paint stripper and bore the ironic title 'Captain Moresby Premium Whisky', and an equivalent number of bottles of altar wine.

An impeccable time for us to venture into talk about politics and whether Bougainville was likely to get its independence. Everyone was confident that Bougainvilleans would vote in overwhelming numbers for independence, but then what would happen? Other countries in the world needed to recognise one's country as independent for it to be a truly independent nation.

'Those bloody Australians don't want us to be independent, that's for sure. All you bloody advisers are about as useful as a rugby team with no ball,' Joseph said, swaying like a prop-forward late on a medals night. As it turned out, he was trialling a line he'd later use in a press release.[2]

As is the wont of the conversations of inebriates, our natters veered off in various unlinked directions before we somehow found ourselves talking about Manus Island, the site where Beatrice's rival, Margaret Mead, did her research, and that served as a major US base during the Second World War. Until 2021, Manus was known for being home to an 'asylum-seeker processing centre' that housed close to 1,000 Afghans, Iranians, Iraqis, and other unfortunates scooped up from boats bound for Australia and

2   Pacific Media Centre Newsdesk, 'Ex-Bougainville VP Blasts Canberra's "Top-Down" Interference in Referendum', *Asia Pacific Report*, 21 August 2018, asiapacificreport.nz/2018/08/21/ex-bougainville-vp-blasts-canberras-top-down-interference-in-referendum/.

dumped on Manus against their will. It was the most wretched, cruel and callous policy imaginable; the aim was to make conditions so awful that it would dissuade future refugees from making the journey.

'You ever heard of Behrouz Boochani?' I asked Joseph.

'How do you spell his name?' he asked and started to look him up on his phone.

Boochani was a Kurdish journalist from northern Iran, then dragooned on Manus. He was writing articles and tweets about the everyday brutalisations he and his fellow detainees suffered in the course of his incarceration. Later, he would write a wondrously expressive book, *No Friend but the Mountains*, the title bearing a dual meaning, referring both to their plight and to a mournful Kurdish adage reflecting the perpetual condition of Boochani's people as a people without a state.[3]

'Bougainvilleans better make sure they have more friends than the mountains,' I said, feeling pleased for drawing what I thought was a searing parallel after our booze cruise. Profundity aside, the reality was that no nation seemed interested in recognising Bougainville as independent; even the referendum itself was advisory in nature, not determinative. Matt Qvortrup, a British academic who visited during my tenure, revealed a memorable finding from his research, which pointed to an unexpectedly strong correlation between the act of holding an independence referendum and actually attaining independence.[4] His finding surprised me. I had assumed the connection would be based on the percentage of votes cast in favour, the peacefulness of the poll and the probity of the process – but it was none of these things. He found that when would-be nations had the backing of at least one permanent member of the Security Council, a 'yea' result in a referendum led to independence. When they didn't, nothing happened. Neither China nor France, Russia nor the United Kingdom, nor the United States seemed very interested in Bougainville, nor did any other country. I often thought that Bougainville's best chance of getting independence rested on courting China in the hope that this would have the effect of enticing other countries to pay more attention to them. Both Eddie and Joseph had been to China, Eddie as 'bodyguard' to the

3   Behrouz Boochani, *No Friend but the Mountains* (Sydney: Macmillan, 2018).
4   Matt Qvortrup, 'Independence Referendums: History, Practice and Outcomes', *Papua New Guinea National Research Institute Research Report* 2 (2018), pngnri.org/images/Publications/Independence-Referendums2.pdf.

president and Joseph on a number of occasions on what he twinklingly called 'sightseeing tours'. We jabbered ramblingly on for another hour before I called it quits. 'The next trip we make we go to the stone pillars,' said Joseph, and I stumbled onto the MV *Salty Eyes* for the sober boatman to ride me home, back to Sohano. We rounded the Tchibo Rock once more, and I recovered from my hangover three days later.

13

Institutions new and old, seen and unseen

> The culture of these people is disappearing with increasing rapidity, and their ideas on every subject are being changed day by day through contact with those of our own civilisation.

Beatrice Blackwood wrote these words in *Both Sides of Buka Passage*. Beatrice chose Bougainville because it had little or no semblance of state administration. Now, the place of which she wrote was gunning to become the world's newest independent nation-state.

In Blackwood's day, Buka boasted just a couple of Chinese-run trade stores by the water's edge, from which she bought sticks of tobacco, betel nuts and bolts to trade for insights. Buka still had something of a trading-outpost feel. The Chinese stores were still here, selling no end of eclectic stuff, such as the bicycle Joseph had bought for Eddie, and the disco tumblers. The store names had catchy but slightly off-base names like 'Happy Sound' and 'New Households Supermarket'. I marvelled at the things that would emerge from shipping containers: car batteries, hair dye ('Africa's best'), plastic shoes, plastic statuettes of Jesus and the saints, face cream that purported to lighten the skin, and an aftershave called 'Angela's choice' that smelled of turpentine. There were noodles, biscuits, soft drinks and a dazzling array of tinned meat, which, in descending order of acquired taste, comprised corned beef, spam, meatloaf, chicken slice and a hideous concoction in a green can styled as 'roasted goose'. Some of the stores had freezers containing chicken, sausages and a cut of meat known as 'flaps'. In all my time there, I feared the answer too much to ever ask which part of the animal 'flaps' emanated from. There was an end-of-the-line feature to some of the Australian canned produce on the shelf: out-of-date jars of pickled onions, home-brand cans of tuna and baked beans.

In addition to the Chinese trading stores, there was a bakery, about 20 beer stores, about 10 dingy restaurants with saveloy sausages and chalky bananas in the warmers, a handful of hotels and the Adventist bookshop that sold *Both Sides of Buka Passage*. The most surreal feature, which arrived soon after I did, was a giant video screen rigged up by the United Nations, which pumped out day-and-night video messages about peace and the referendum, in a manner faintly reminiscent of Orwell's *1984*. Beside the screen was a 'referendum information office', which was always closed. For those more interested in night life, it could be found on the way to the airport at Club Oasis, a nightclub where seats in the VIP room looked like tulips and which was owned by Bougainville's minister for economic development, who also owned the island's only sports car.

What would an anthropologist like Beatrice Blackwood have made of the work I was doing each day on both sides of Buka Passage? There were times I thought that I had assembled enough material for a book on the impersonations, roles and magical properties ascribed to a ghost-like form that people referenced often, invested zealous faith in but rarely ever saw. It was called the government, and she would have been as fascinated as I was by the way in which the government went about its daily business.

What would have especially fascinated Beatrice the anthropologist was just how much Bougainvilleans had metabolised all the appurtenances of bureaucratic language and development speak, but with less of the form. More than a few public servants claimed they couldn't work effectively without job descriptions but seldom developed them. The region's Cabinet – the Executive Council – met regularly, but notes were not always taken of their deliberations, which meant no-one knew what was agreed. Sometimes it felt as if a plan or MoU was insisted upon as being a prerequisite for every conceivable activity but was not always implemented after being prepared, the document itself sinking into an a mass of paper on some shelf.

A few weeks after my booze cruise with Eddie and Joseph, the government held a meeting to review its Strategic Development Plan 2018–22. The plan – developed entirely by fellow consultants, adorned with pictures of expectant children and coming in at over 100 pages – was certainly ambitious. It set more than 300 expansive and complex tasks for the government to accomplish, ranging from developing a database of veterans (such as Eddie) to building hospitals, to the development of geospatial databases. The 'bureaucrat' to 'complex task' ratio was less than 2:1. The title of the review meeting was a bingo card of buzzwords: 'Review and Alignment Workshop: Strengthening Bougainville's Governance Framework Through Partnerships to Achieve Socio-Economic & Infrastructure Development', and naturally it was supported by 'donor partners'. The meeting was held at the Kuri resort, another joint down by the waterfront that had a tiny pool housing three giant turtles.

The meeting began an hour and a half late. Following songs from a high school choir, the man who had the title of 'Deputy Chief, Policy and Planning, Office of the President & the Bougainville Executive Council' opened proceedings. He was a former senior officer in the defence force who preferred to be known by his military designation. He looked every inch the picture-dictionary definition of a public servant; he was always impeccably dressed in a plaid shirt, well-knotted tie and trousers held up by an RM Williams belt.

He spoke sonorously and began by telling the assembled public servants that he was putting them 'on notice'. The first slide of his presentation showed a squashed-face emoji sitting atop the image of a glitter ball from a 1980s discotheque, inside of which was written the word 'SITUATION'. To the right of the glitter ball was a purple arrow with the word 'JOURNEY', written using an eye-catching Rastafarian colour scheme, at the end point of which was a sunflower petal with the word 'IDEAL' in a differently sized font. Below it, the text proclaimed: 'We make the plan of our journey to make the situation to become the ideal'. The next slide was of a large set of tubular pipes reminiscent of a cathedral organ, over which were written bureaucratic words like 'Target/Short-Term Goal', 'Logic', 'Vision/Impact', 'Annual Report' and 'Director'.

The 20-minute presentation went on for an hour. Not once did he refer to the actual contents of the extensively put-together plan. I desperately wanted to ask the man about the logic of his circumlocutory presentation, but no-one else asked him any questions, and I didn't think it my place to. Indeed, there were lots of appreciative nods. 'We will start reviewing this plan on Monday,' he thundered. He didn't. And in the weeks that followed, no-one seemed surprised.

I thought often of my predecessors in this and other adjacent positions. In the dining room of one of Buka's hotels was a pinboard on which were affixed hundreds of business cards of people who had gone before me, people with mysterious titles like 'senior strategic adviser', 'economic development counsellor', 'partnership coordinator'; one didn't need to go too far to discover the wellspring for all these visions of state being adopted by the Bougainville government. I'd go and have fish soup and white bread there some lunchtimes and look at these cards, wondering what imprints all those people had made, what indelible marks I was making.

There were about 15 of us working on this program of support to the government. We each had our quirks, our foibles and our egos. Some of us were, I'm sure, here because we didn't want to be somewhere else; some were paying off a mortgage, while others reminded me of a comment in *A Passage to India* made by the protagonist, Cyril Fielding: 'I'm delighted to be here ... There's my only excuse.'[1]

Like Beatrice going off into the unknown, we had our handbooks, which emphasised the importance of developing policies, plans and procedures. We were all engaged in the same necromancy, trying to conjure up a government through the production of ever more complex plans and detailed policies.

I felt like a taxi idling at Buka airport for a short town-trip when there are, at the most, a couple of flights a day. I'd outgrown my time in Buka. Few were interested in the legal-rational advice that was our faith: let's look at what the constitution says, let's look at what the regulations say, let's work out how to draft a submission outlining the issues. I found myself starting to feel like Blackwood near the end of her stay, chasing some sort of knowledge I truly didn't need.

Too many days felt inordinate, and often I felt I engaged in as much clockwatching as public servants, clicking on the send/receive button in the faint hope of being occupied. I became so weepingly upset one day following an inadvertent breach of 'protocols' that a colleague prayed over me to give me God's grace. I started writing a murder mystery novel that began with an expatriate government adviser being found with a copy of a policy constricting his throat. Apart from my brief, incomplete foray

---

1   Edward Morgan Forster and Oliver Stallybrass, *A Passage to India* (London, Penguin: 2000), 124.

into mystery writing, the slow pace certainly gave me lots of time to read, but that liberty would occasionally reinforce my melancholy. I was suffering myself from what Everest-Phillips described as bureaupathology.

One morning, when I was scrolling around Twitter, I came across a review of a memoir called *Rascal Rain*, which quoted the author, Inez Baranay, as saying that the book was the hardest piece of writing she had ever engaged in.[2] The topic seemed apposite to my surroundings, as it related to her experiences working within a local government area elsewhere in PNG. The account certainly contains some amusing, picaresque detail typical of the genre: the clapped-out printer, the absentee staff, the outrageous expenses claims and an all-permeating aura of resigned resentment. But there is a deep sadness to Baranay's book, as well – a sense that she herself was failing. I sympathised. I empathised.

An afterword recalls how upset Baranay felt by the reaction to her work; reviewers of her book castigated her for cultural imperialism and for being insufficiently respectful of 'culture'. To me, the book read like a woman writing unsparingly about what she saw and felt, but it also exposed the dangers of writing. She wrote the equivalent of Blackwood's letters and paid the price.

Baranay's reality was sometimes our reality, which we wrote about in the modern-day equivalent of Beatrice's letters: WhatsApp messages to each other. We worked for the equivalent of what Beatrice had excoriated: 'They're all scared stiff of the emissaries of the League of Nations, who know nothing of the conditions here but lay down all sorts of impossible strictures and limitations.' For 'League of Nations', read Canberra, New York, Wellington. The very style of reporting that was required – arid, adhering always to a technical plan – did not enable disclosure of the very real, often unplanned and sometimes unexpected victories that emerged in the course of the long durée.

Occasionally, some people from past pursuits showed up for a week or so: consultants working in peacebuilding and conflict resolution, academics topping up salaries and chasing relevance by drafting research reports. We'd meet down at Reasons, where the pizza oven was still below the stairs, or in the lodge with the old business cards. It was always fun to catch up with the visitors. Bougainville was slowly emerging as a topic

2   Baranay, *Rascal Rain*.

of interest with the referendum edging closer, but I often felt we had neither the syntax nor the vocabulary to describe what was going on. Ingrained in the domain of the academic is the need to reach evidence-based conclusions, develop sets of recommendations for what should happen, and triumphantly draft an article or report that they were certain would be read and actioned – to see the world as an entirely logical domain. There was less about how to deal with the complexities of the ordinary, the mundane occurrences of the everyday: what to do about absenteeism, petty jealousies, the heat in the offices being so great that it induced lethargic doldrums, the pressures of having family members coming asking for money, and the interwoven effects of these and many other factors. The visitors were here to help, we were here to help – but were we helping?

* * *

I went for a dusk walk around the little 15-minute looped walking track on Sohano, passing the old adviser house where I had first lodged, and skirting the yapping, snarling dogs at the turn of the small incline. To my right was a Japanese Zero on its plinth, a memorial to that country's war dead, overlooking the Tchibo rock in Buka Passage. Further along the track were a Marian shrine, a rusted car and, to the left of wide-canopied trees filled with flying foxes, the old Buka hospital, which now housed the Department of Health. The final landmark on my circuit was the row of raised houses where many of the ministers that made up the Bougainville government lived with their families. I was trying to puzzle out in my head the goings-on of the Strategic Development Plan meeting, turning over what an anthropologist would make of it, searching for paragraphs and words for ways to understand the performance of this government, with its precisionist phraseologies of corporate plans, strategic plans and sector plans, when I stopped in my tracks. To my right, sitting on a rock and staring at the islands in the Solomon Sea beyond, was a teenage boy looking as if he had stepped from a photoframe in *Both Sides of Buka Passage.*

The boy was wearing an *upe* of purple and ochre, and I resisted the temptation to whip out my iPhone and take a picture of him as if he were an exhibit in a zoo. I lacked Beatrice's chutzpah. When I walked around for another loop, the boy had gone.

This faintest of encounters made me think that I was getting it all wrong, or at the very least, I was missing an important part of the big picture. In being too close to the ragtag pantomime of the administration, I was missing an appreciation of all the proceedings that were occurring backstage, all the things that were hidden from my eyes.

Seeing the boy made a connection with a book I had enjoyed deeply some months prior. The book was *Underland*,[3] an exploration by the British nature writer Robert Macfarlane of the worlds beneath our feet, worlds that we don't privilege because we don't tangibly perceive them. In one of the most memorable sections of the book, Macfarlane travels deep underground to a laboratory where scientists are trying to use tools to discern dark matter, an element that science recognises as existing – estimates vary, but it makes up approximately 30 per cent of the Earth. Despite this, scientists still struggle to develop the tools to be able to glimpse it, never mind plot out its topographical lines and contours.

Thinking about Macfarlane's description of dark matter, and the boy-becoming-a-man wearing the *upe,* started to make me acutely aware of all the things around me in Bougainville that I didn't have the instruments to see.

I thought of the household where I was now boarding, adjacent to the old adviser house. Head of the household was Ralph Christensen, a man who would not have existed without the mine, because without it there is little likelihood that his parents could have met. His father was Swiss-German and had come to work in Panguna; his mother was from Buin, in southern Bougainville. Brought up in Arawa, Ralph attended boarding school in Brisbane and served an apprenticeship in a Michelin-starred kitchen in Geneva. He was Buka's serial entrepreneur, a man in perpetual motion, and he spoke nineteen to the dozen about his business plans. Ralph owned the town's bakery and its meat-pie shop, which was located beside the Hot Rooster, and he had a Roman candle of diverse business interests: fisheries, minerals, refrigeration, construction and a barge that crossed the Buka Passage. He was also the owner of the region's only jet ski, hopping on which was the highlight of my kids' visit to Bougainville. I liked Ralph. We were the same age, but he was already, to use the old saw, well on the way to becoming a Buka institution.

---

3   Robert Macfarlane, *Underland: A Deep Time Journey* (London: Penguin Books, 2019).

His was no nuclear household. Along with Ralph's wife, Judith, and four children there was a sizeable cast of people who stayed and worked in their home, all related in some way: John the gardener; Philomena the general factotum and de-facto 'housekeeper'; Ezron the boatman; and a rotating-cast crew down at the dock on Sohano and on the scrubby patch of waste ground down by the Buka waterfront to which Ezron would scoot back and forth multiple times each day, his last nightly journey ferrying over his father, Peter, who was manager at the bakery, to bring back the day's takings. Ralph employed hundreds in his businesses, all of whom were connected through kin or recommended by kin, part of wider clan networks. Ralph's set-up wasn't formalised: no-one had a formal job description, no-one adhered to a quarterly plan, yet it was a much more organised and effective institution than anything officially deemed governmental in Bougainville.

In the Sisyphean work I was involved with in Bougainville, 'institutions' was synonymous with government institutions, but I would come to see this as too narrow a definition because it focused solely on what could be *seen*, what occupied a concrete space, what could be lamented for its absence. It didn't cover what I couldn't see. As Sinclair Dinnen, who had worked with me in Bougainville all those years earlier, has observed, 'The analytical separation between academics [and] practitioners' in this line of work 'remains a wide one'. One set treats it as an exercise to be located within a wider historical canvas of thousands of years, and the other as a set of budgeted activities to be judged between the cyclic rhythms of completing the monthly time sheet.[4]

Academics have a much broader definition of institutions than do aid programs. In academia, the most prominent definition of an institution is that of the economist Douglass North, who defined them as 'the humanly devised constraints that structure political, economic, and social interaction'. He continues:

---

4   Sinclair Dinnen, 'A Comment on State-Building in Solomon Islands', *Journal of Pacific History* 42, no. 2 (2007): 255–63, doi.org/10.1080/00223340701461700.

They consist of both informal constraints (sanctions, taboos, customs, traditions, and codes of conduct) and formal rules (constitutions, laws, property rights). Throughout history, institutions have been devised by human beings to create order and reduce uncertainty in exchange.[5]

According to these criteria, the Bougainville government's institutions were just one type among many, and far from being the most important. It's just that the others weren't visible, didn't organise themselves into glossy brochures with ministerial forewords that the likes of me would pen. One of the most important 'dark matter' institutions is the clan system that stretches over the length and breadth of Bougainville, cutting across its 21 distinct languages, eight sublanguages and 39 dialects.[6] Anthropologists who followed in Beatrice's shoes would map its outlines, rules and strictures, and observe its complexity. None ever seemed to feel they got their descriptions entirely right.

Like the *upe*-wearing boy that evening, these institutions only revealed themselves glancingly and incompletely: carvings of clan symbols resembling hornbills and eagles on the boats at Pororan, Joseph on his plastic chair, adjudicating supplicants at the *Salty Eyes*, meetings that Eddie would drop everything for and head off to, threaded bonds of those who had fought together in the resistance, the churches whose services always started on time.

It also helped explain why other parts of the program in which I worked – parts provided grants for water and sanitation projects and the like – seemed to be faring much better in terms of impact and effectiveness. For a start, they were delivering something tangible and needed, but they were also working *with* the grain of actual institutions, i.e. the leadership structures at the community level. We, by contrast, were working with an 'institution' that was less substantial, less well founded, and alien in terms of its hierarchies and ostensible goals.

---

5   Douglass C. North, 'Institutions', *Journal of Economic Perspectives* 5, no. 1 (Winter, 1991): 97, doi.org/10.1257/jep.5.1.97.

6   Anthony J. Regan, 'Bougainville: Beyond Survival', *Cultural Survival Quarterly Magazine*, September 2002, culturalsurvival.org/publications/cultural-survival-quarterly/bougainville-beyond-survival.

Just because I couldn't see much of these local institutions with my eyes didn't mean that these institutions weren't there. It's just that I could see them only indistinctly, if at all. I simply wasn't a full member of the clan, and I was too immersed in my own rites and ceremonies, ones that I was seeing ever less reason to have faith in.

The political scientist Volker Boege has called Bougainville a 'hybrid political order',[7] a distinct variety of 'peace' and 'State', one that is a mix-and-match between institutional forms. Boege was drawing on a deep well of scholarship. Joel Migdal,[8] whose work *Strong Societies and Weak States* I read when I was at college, wrote about the struggles of administrations to become *the* institutions in society because the informal ones all around them are stronger. Other scholars have been writing about other parts of Melanesia in similar terms for years. But this all points to a gloomy epiphany. There are articles and books that sketch out how places like Bougainville operate, but we are not always willed to put that understanding to much practical use.

* * *

In the spirit of Beatrice's anthropology, I decided one day to find out if there was an origin story behind the most prized piece of apparel in Bougainville: the death metal T-shirt. To be sporting a fresh Korn, Slayer or similar T-shirt, or a picture of a skeleton marching out of the grave, was a sign of status and prestige. My research approach was less methodologically exacting than that of Beatrice: I put out a call on social media and asked for help in boosting my understanding. I knew of bands named Black Ops and the Blackout Band, but what were the names of others? My knowledge increased: others were called Ozium, Dishonoured, Shadowfools, Living Death, War X, Flag of War and Tatai Force Aquafire, the last of which, when I listened to them, sounded like the soundtrack to a military coup. The government's chief of protocol, a neighbour on Sohano, was the drummer in another band, Mortal Revenge; his Saturday afternoon practices stress-tested my noise-cancelling headphones.

---

7   Volker Boege, 'Hybridisation of Peacebuilding at the Local–International Interface: The Bougainville Case', in *Hybridity on the Ground in Peacebuilding and Development: Critical Conversations*, ed. Joanne Wallis et al., (Canberra: ANU Press, 2018), 115–28, doi.org/10.22459/hgpd.03.2018.07.
8   Joel S. Migdal, *Strong Societies and Weak States: State–Society Relations and State Capabilities in the Third World* (Princeton, NJ: Princeton University Press, 1988).

'You ever seen the meme about the Bougainville starter kit?' Ken Imako asked me one day over Zoom. 'Essential items are a Metallica T-shirt, some big safety boots and a backpack.' I hadn't really thought of the prevalence of steel-capped workman's boots until he mentioned it, but it was true. I'd been introduced to Ken through Twitter. He was the drummer in DarkAsidE, the name a damned good play on words.

We had arranged a Zoom chat. I expected to see him in Bougainville but found him in his spare room in Brisbane with a giant set of drums in the background. Ken was an arbitration lawyer in his early forties and had moved to Brisbane with his wife. As a child he had been evacuated to Port Moresby just as the Crisis began and was educated in the capital. It was just before Christmas; he had a grizzled holiday beard, was wearing a Nirvana T-shirt and reminded me of a younger Paul Giamatti.

Ken thought the preponderance of death metal was another legacy of the mine:

> A lot of the workers that came to Bougainville were blue-collar types and brought with them albums of now-forgotten Aussie pub rock like The Rose Tap and The Angels. The mineworkers left and the music stayed. These bands were like a gateway drug, and we moved onto harder things: AC/DC, Metallica, Slayer. With the music came the fashion associated with it. So … in addition to the music being brought in, from the mineworkers came the fashion. The jackets started off with the flares, you know, the bell bottoms and skinny jeans so tight that they threatened impotence to the wearer.

> It's … like we latched onto it from that point. It's always, sort of, been in the blood. It's fascinating to me now that, you know, a lot of the kids still wear those types of clothes, but they don't listen to the music. It's just another way of setting us apart.[9]

I forgot to ask Ken about the equally ubiquitous red bandanas: certainly some pub rock antecedents influenced that apparel, but I wondered how much Sylvester Stallone's bandana-wearing character Rambo may have had something to do with it, too.

---

9   Ken Imako, in an online conversation with the author, December 2020.

As far as my musical preferences go, I am more of an alt-country, stuck-in-the-1980s type of person, and I asked for starter music to try to get across metal. It made me feel old; I started to sound like my father, complaining that I couldn't hear the lyrics for all the strangulated din. One of the few songs in which I could discern the words was Metallica's 'Enter Sandman', in which they sing about going 'to never-never land'. It struck a chord. From the lost generation to the empty words of 'becoming the ideal' presentation, gaps in knowledge, understanding and resources abounded. Yet, what was lacking was compensated by an unerring sense that independence was the right thing to aspire to. While we advisers and aid workers bustled about, 'working hard' on things that were hardly working, Bougainvilleans and their 'underland' institutions could see a never-never land that we simply could not.

PART THREE

It was what our ancestors wanted.
— Eddie Mohin

14

Odd jobs, family trips and a friend worth fighting for

Even when Suzanne's posting ended, I remained engaged with Bougainville, as well as taking on other projects elsewhere in PNG. I would go for shorter stints, joining the Monday morning salmon-run flights up to Port Moresby with a cabin full of fellow consultants, bankers, miners and the occasional researcher. I thought of how in earlier times, PNG was a destination for the young and the spry, but now it was more a haunt for greying men with more yesterdays than they had tomorrows. Comfortably less than 10 per cent of the people on each flight were women. About the same percentage were Papua New Guinean.

In Port Moresby I worked for a spell as a consultant with the department responsible for administering the country's complicated system of local government, the multiple layers of which resembled trifle. They construed this task as setting up committees that never met, copying and pasting old documents into new ones and giving Jesuitical answers to straight questions. It reminded me of trying to play Scrabble with a wearisome opponent without a dictionary prior to the advent of the internet, the sort of person who would claim 'BGDSY' was a proper word because there was no evidence to the contrary. Some things didn't much differ, including the same disturbing problem – which was quite rational, if you thought about it – of only being able to rouse the staff with a prospect of a 'field trip' fully inclusive of flights, generous travel allowance and accommodation. Or, if it were a day to be held in situ, woe betide the planners if they didn't set it up in the Lamana Hotel, all repast included, and no expectation that anyone would be either present or operational until after morning tea. (The Lamana is a colonnaded hotel complex painted in a shimmering white, with a Graeco-Roman-meets-Pablo Escobar vibe, a step up from the Holiday Inn. Until recently, it hosted female mud-wrestling competitions.)

But it was we who were the true dupes. No matter how little interest departmental employees would evince, how passive-aggressively we'd be rebuffed, how much we'd be disparaged on social media for being stupid white people, like eager beagles we'd come back for more. I did some other work with the justice program and marvelled at the indefatigable work of some of the old hands – expats and Papua New Guineans – who worked on it, all exponents of the dogged *brukim bus* approach to work, accepting the non-linear, stop-start nature of change, knowing how much can be cultivated and how much is beyond the immediate control of the program. This work was intangible: phone calls returned, softly spoken advice taken, reports that would not otherwise be written being finalised with encouragement, meetings held and acknowledgement of the other institutions at play. Much of this humble, quiet work cannot be easily summarised in terms of reference; much of it is hard for any one adviser to reflect upon in the course of all the reports that were the regular banes of their lives. I wrote a long report about these individuals working steadfastly in the trenches for a contracting company; sadly, I have little or no idea whatever happened to it; presumably it was flung into some long-forgotten gyre of overlooked scribing.

During many of these assignments, I'd stay at the Holiday Inn, which reminded me of the setting of Graham Greene's *A Burnt Out Case* in terms of its meta-narrative about how tropical lassitude wearies the soul. Many of the denizens of the hotel's Gekko Bar would have fitted in well in a 21st-century reboot. There was the government minister watching himself on the television above the bar in a news story about launching of a corporate plan, nodding in approbation at the sagacity of his words, and the grey-haired man who tackled a bottle of sauvignon blanc solo while typing furiously on his laptop. Most of the times I went there, I also saw a few members of the Bougainville government lounging around next to the swimming pool with its downward slope as acute as the mountain screes surrounding the city.

On one uneventful night, I had a memorable conversation. I had been reading the newspaper, which contained its usual fare: the announcement of a new framework; the signing of yet another MoU; an arcane parliamentary stoush over whether a safari suit constituted appropriate dress within the chamber, when the glassy-eyed white man next to me asked, apropos of nothing, 'You still here?' A woman more than 40 years his junior who had been his drinking companion had left. Close to finishing his beer, he motioned to one of the wait staff, always dressed in tennis whites, to fetch him another bottle. He was in his mid-sixties, I reckoned, paunchy like a kangaroo with a joey, and wore a chain of keycards around his neck reminiscent of the old pictures of chiefs with their collars of pigs' teeth. His bulbous nose looked like a navigation map to one of Papua New Guinea's great river deltas. He wore a blue business shirt and a pair of football shorts, the sartorial incongruity of which reminded me of one of those choose-your-own-uniform flip books my kids had when they were little. On nodding terms over the years, we had never spoken before. Where I grew up in Northern Ireland, the first question was always aimed at determining what religion you were. In the Gekko, it was how long you'd been here. His beer had loosened him up.

'Yep,' I replied, 'but just a short trip this time. I'm finishing up and going home tomorrow. I'm a bit tired of all this going back and forth, and there are days when you really wonder whether all this … stuff is really worth it.'

I had had a few loosening lagers by this point, too. 'You'll be back,' he averred. His tone mixed avuncularity with ennui and portent.

'I've had four *go pinis* parties now (referring to leaving parties) but always come back. I don't know why. It drives me up the wall most days. "Just one more year, one more contract," I always say to myself.'

He went on to talk about a holiday in Bali planned for the end of this particular contract. Its purpose, he said, was to 'get it out of my system'. I didn't dare ask what the 'it' in his previous sentence was referencing. I noticed a wedding band on his left hand and asked him if his wife was with him. I figured him for a straight man; he had looked positively lascivious as he followed the behind of his erstwhile companion when she was walking away. 'She's in Melbourne,' he replied:

> I went back home after the last contract ended, and she told me she just didn't want me around the house. 'Just go back up,' she said. She likes the money, but not me anymore.

It was one of the saddest statements I had ever heard. He paused and took another good swig on his bottle. 'I'm one of those people now, you know.'

'Who?' I asked.

'You know, one of those missionaries, misfits and mercenaries that always come here, always running away. Which one are you?'

The conversation unlocked something in me. Our marriage had survived Zimbabwe. I loved my wife and my boys deeply (I still do!), but all this frequent-flyer-point accumulation meant that I wasn't spending as much time with them as I wanted. It dawned on me that this woebegone man's tale was a cautionary one – I needed to not lock myself into this life.

As the boys grew out of babyhood, they had come to join me during the school holidays and got to know some of the friends and personalities I had made during my time. They particularly liked Bougainville; they loved the Lilliputian smallness of Buka Town, the friendliness of everyone they met, and the short rides across the passage to and from Sohano in Ezron's motorised skiff. One time, an old lady came up to me in the Buka market and asked if she could take a photo of herself with them. I asked her why. She said she hadn't seen a 'white child' in Buka since the late eighties.

The boys also stayed at the Holiday Inn, so they frequently suggested that they, too, should get a slice of the reward points I was accruing. I'd bring them into the NCOBA building and park them in offices with books and an iPad, and the staff would keep an eye on them while I'd do – I don't know what.

They were coming up so regularly that my friend and colleague Dennis Kuiai would refer to them as the 'junior consultants' and chide me when I told them to shush when they were larking around. 'In Melanesia,' he'd say, 'a noisy child means a happy child.' It was when they were quiet that I should take notice, he told me, because children could sense untoward spirits which adults could not. The boys delighted in having permission to make a ruckus, and I often thought of Andersen's *The Emperor's New Clothes* when they were with me. When they asked me what all my long meetings were *actually* about, I struggled to give a convincing answer.

Dennis was also a large part of the reason why I stayed engaged – he was someone worth supporting. I can remember vividly the first time I met Dennis, up at a school hall just outside of Buka. It was about a month after I first arrived, and there was a 'Leadership Summit' to discuss what to do about the referendum. Speaker after speaker would take to the stage and deliver impassioned oratory about the need for work to be done.

The former president of Autonomous Region of Bougainville, James Tanis, introduced us to each other. I remember the torque in Dennis's handshake and a query forming in the irises of his eyes as to whether this person was worth investing any time in. I'm glad he thought that I was. He was a tall man whose walk revealed, faintly, the legacy of the injured foot that he had once walked with, repaired by two Bougainvillean doctors at Buka General Hospital. The operation was a success, but Dennis's feet were still in such a condition that he wore sandals daily, and his left foot was always taped to cover sores that had never fully healed after the operation.

Our minds worked in similar ways: finding out paths by asking questions, going to documents to see what they said in black and white rather than just making something up. He had a keen mind that always sought to learn more. He wrote, and he wrote well. He would write long, detailed documents that he'd send on to his minister. He'd sign the letters he wrote in a distinctive way: 'In the Service of Our People'. He wrote papers; he loved to have his thinking challenged. He came prepared to meetings, read voraciously and always relished an opportunity to correct my written English. He had a developed knowledge of the Peace Agreement. What I valued also about Dennis was his realism. His dream was independence, too, but he was practical enough to know that it couldn't just be wished up, as in a letter to Santa. It would require hard, boring, assiduous, nuts-and-bolts work.

Dennis was a Swiss Army knife not only in a bureaucratic sense: he worked on collecting some of the weapons still in Bougainville,[1] trying to engage Eddie and his cohort so they felt included, drafting concrete ideas as a basis for substantive discussions with PNG, dampening down frustrations that bubbled up among the veterans with Bougainville's stingy peace.

He had taken over the department in Buka after his predecessor was dismissed. Formally, his office was inside one of the administration's old dongas, but his receiving room and operations centre was a piece of concrete wall half-shaded from the beating sun by a tiny, overhanging

---

1   McKenna, 'Status and Implementation', 19–23.

ledge next to the giant pothole; it was beside a shipping container filled with papers thrown in randomly over the years and constituting the government's archive.

Dennis was far from the only hard worker in the administration at Buka. There were others I worked with whose work ethic and drive I admired tremendously: Ephraim, for example, a young man who worked with Dennis and who always seemed to be overlooked for trips to Port Moresby because he wasn't connected enough; Zoe and Rooney at the Lands Department; and a young woman called Daphne, whom we coaxed and coached regularly to have faith in herself. We once spent half a day helping Daphne organise her thoughts into a speech for that unforgettable 'strategic planning alignment review workshop' – George and I played the equivalent of judges on a talent show to rate her practice performances, and she delivered on stage with aplomb. I loved working with these people; they relished being challenged and given alternative ways to think about issues, inspiring in me the will to do my best by them.

Still, it was no easy place to work, as the rise and fall of Joseph Nobetau showed. Nobetau served as Bougainville's chief secretary from late 2016 to August 2019. He was from the southern town of Buin, close to the bottom point of the main island and the sea border with Solomon Islands. A former diplomat, Nobetau had previously been Papua New Guinea's acting chief migration officer. The arc of his career as chief secretary can be charted in the compendium of press releases, updates and reports he published during his tenure, which are, inexplicably given his fate, still on the website of the government that would go on to dismiss him. Unlike the official reports I was writing, which were very much of the 'on-the-one-hand-and-on-the-other' school of exposition, Nobetau's reports were written with the feather-ruffling abandon of a man in charge.

In his dispatches from his early months he strikes a glass-half-full approach. According to his first quarterly report,[2] his early work is 'already showing dividends', notwithstanding 'immense challenges'. But after a few months, the enormity of the task he has taken on emerges. By his second report, he is writing about the 'number of individuals and groups within the public service actively engaging in disruptive and corrupt activities' and notes the apparent sense that government is too often envisioned as a piggybank from which to take money as and when the whim arises.

---

2   The first and second quarterly reports are on file with the author.

He notes the culture of claims: public servants putting in receipts for vehicle hire, cash advances, phone credit and 'travel to the Holiday Inn for frivolous reasons'. He says to a gathering of public servants: 'The reality is that many of our public servants don't do as much as they should. In fact, some just don't bother coming to work'.

Nobetau undertakes an audit of the payroll to find a 'Murder on the Orient Express'-style scenario in which many of the public servants have been the beneficiaries of additional allowances. He discovers 'ghost workers' on the payroll, sucking out funds in excess of over 18 million kina (just over A\$7 million) per annum. He refers six departmental secretaries for investigation; Board of Inquiry member Ila later finds there are causes to dismiss all but one of them for various rorts involving allowances and expenses.

This Frank-Serpico-of-the-South-Seas routine won Nobetau no friends. Politicians can talk about going after corruption in the abstract, but when the people being booted out, suspended or placed at risk of being visited by the Fraud Squad are your kin, your cousins or your brothers or sisters, and one worries whether the next policeman's knock might be for you, then nothing is likely to dissipate your fulsome support faster. The politicians went on to dismiss Nobetau for being guilty of an offence not on any known statute book: 'undermining Bougainville unity'. (In 2020, a court found that his sacking was unconstitutional.)

* * *

As 2019 began, I found myself spending less time in Bougainville itself and more of my allocated time in Port Moresby. I was there to participate in something grandly called a 'Post-Referendum Planning Task Force'.

The idea behind the initiative was sound: it foresaw the two governments getting together to work out what would happen to this corner of the country once the vote occurred, and to prepare for the constitutionally mandated post-referendum consultations. This touched on other important matters.

What would be the attributes of an independent Bougainville, if that were to be the choice at the referendum? What would be the attributes of Bougainville if it had greater autonomy, which was the other choice before voters? How long would a transition take? How could Bougainville finance itself?

The question of finances was crucial. A three-day, necessarily tedious tax and revenue summit had been held on the matter in 2017, but the technical recommendations had gone unheeded. Instead, the government was fixated on get-rich schemes. These schemes rolled on; they included a Bougainville airline, a seaweed business and investment in one of the Chinese supermarkets in Buka Town. (The latter certainly benefited the owner of the store; one day he closed up and took whatever money he'd made with him.) Close to the end of my stay, an Australian who bred Arabian horses came in with a proposal to take over the mine.

The format for this task force was a good one. 'Technical officers' would meet first, then prepare documents for politicians, who would make decisions. The problem was that, save for the industrious Dennis and a handful of others, not enough technical officers had the technical knowledge to make decisions, nor did they come prepared, so every meeting took on a quality as circular as the tables we were meeting at. Meetings started hours late; we would then break for 'morning tea', which quickly morphed into lunch. The politicians would make oratory statements such as, 'We need to make decisions as leaders,' but they rarely did. This was reinforcing dysfunction once again, and bedecking the event in a grand title obscured only some of these troubling realities.

The meetings would be held at the city's grand International Conference Centre, built by the Chinese a few years previously in advance of a multination summit. For reasons I didn't pretend to fathom, some of the Chinese staff seemed to stay on with the building long after the summit was a distant bureaucratic memory. It always fascinated me as to what their actual role must be. On most of the days we met, one of them would arrive in the room clutching an old-fashioned camera, take a few snaps and leave. I'd love to know what they did with those photos; did they append them to breezy reports back to Beijing reporting how the building was still being used for important meetings, or were such reports more analytical, describing events as they were?

Certainly, an honest accounting of those times would note the nature of such meetings, whose focus was on pedantic technicalities. Objections were raised to things previously agreed; no-one had all the documentation, and the relevant people frequently didn't show up. 'A wonderful week of progress', the reps from the United Nations, responsible for sponsoring the event, acclaimed. The UN had engaged the services of two facilitators, who flew in from London and Manila; and leaving aside the usual effects of jet lag, it's probable they felt foggy throughout. Each month they'd set tasks for 'technical officers' to undertake, and each month there'd be a beautifully constructed and implausible reason why less had been accomplished than had been expected.

I thought often of FR Stockwell when I sat in the back row of this cavernous room. Stockwell was a 'Queen and Country' man of the old school, station chief in Cairo and Khartoum after the war, and the grandfather of a friend of mine who writes historical crime novels.[3] Stockwell had a wonderful maxim about political meetings:

> Decide before you have a meeting whether it is meant to achieve anything substantive. If it isn't, hold it in a good hotel. If it is, hold it in the desert, at noon, with no shade, and nowhere to sit.

Stockwell would have known the pack drill for this sort of meeting well. Around and around we'd go on the same old okey-doke, the minute hand on the clock pushing slowly upstream.

* * *

It was when I got the notification I'd been upgraded to platinum-elite status that I knew for sure I'd been spending way too much time in the Holiday Inn. I could feel my belt tightening from a combination of hash browns and Gekko house wine, and my lips felt a little chapped from too many scalding flat whites sourced from the hotel's belching self-serve coffee machine. I could feel my languor rising, looking around at so many others engaging in forlorn pursuits. Change was in the air for Bougainville as the referendum neared, and for me it was a sign that I, too, was shifting out of that to which I'd perhaps become too habituated. But I wanted to stay to see what was going to happen.

---

3   Dominck Donald, 'Dominick Donald Thriller Writer', dominickdonald.com.

15

Referendum days

After various delays, the referendum took place throughout two weeks in late November and early December 2019. I arrived in the middle of the first week to find little Buka Town enjoying its place in the sun. 'CNN, BBC, the Australians – they have all been here,' said a man who came up to me at the market, hoping I was a journalist and that he could be interviewed. He was disappointed to find out I wasn't. I asked his forecast for the eventual result. He was sure it was going to be a thumping majority for independence and repeated a similar version to Eddie's and Joseph's arguments: riches on the land and in the sea, and good times ahead.

The little town was spruced up beyond recognition. Grass verges had been trimmed, and the storm drains long clogged with cans and bottles, and coated with red betel nut expectorant, as well as Christ knows what else, had been cleaned up. Even the giant crater in the middle of the main government offices had been filled in and the sliding gate repaired. It was a tangible demonstration of how much Bougainvilleans could accomplish and how judging the place on the performance of its inert government alone would be a mistake.

It felt like a nation-in-waiting.

The Bougainville flag was everywhere. It flew from lamp posts and cars, from every cranny of every ramshackle building in town. The Chinese owners of 'Hot Rooster' had put two flags on either side of the chicken that was dressed in a blue majorette's uniform, giving two thumbs up. Even the inflatable 10-foot-high Santa Claus outside the pharmacy had one tucked in between the fold of his thumb and index finger. The flag was inscribed onto earrings and necklaces and stuck onto the front of sunglasses in positions so prominent as to half blind the wearer. Comfortably 50 per cent of the town was wearing various black acrylic T-shirts that bore the flag, along with proud appellations such as 'Black Power', 'Black Pearl of the Pacific' and 'Land of the Blacks'. I bought some T-shirts for myself and my two sons – all 'Made in China' – in one of the small stalls in the little park in the centre of town.

Beside the park was the most extraordinary cloth banner depicting the gold head of a Babylonian king, a purple body, brass-coloured thighs and legs of clay, representing the Holy Roman Empire. It was quite the most extraordinary banner I have ever seen. The preacher who used to bellow sometimes at the market had erected it, and I went to ask him where he got it. He told me it was a gift from God.

I found the referendum to be exceptionally well organised and managed, an opinion reinforced by the positive comments coming from the large range of observer missions that fanned out across the region during the two-week polling period.[1] Each night, hundreds of people would gather with flags outside the police station as trucks, creaky buses and little flotillas of boats brought in the ballot boxes from polling stations all around the region, where they were to be stored in the safe beside the cells, after closure of the polling stations, until counting began. Down near Kurtatchi, young men came out from clearings within the forest wearing their *upe* to cast ballots before heading straight back into the glades. There was a sense of this being the most important and cathartic of community and political events, a culmination of a process many years in the making.[2] Throughout Buka, little Catholic shrines and crosses had been repainted and lights affixed to them. 'Joyous' and 'excited' aren't the first adjectives to reach for to describe Buka Town, but they were the descriptors that best encompassed the mood during those referendum days.

Moreover, this joy was fuelled by nothing more than soft drinks and coconuts. Anyone looking for beer, altar wine, that rasping Captain Moresby whiskey or even a swig of home brew was out of luck. A booze ban was in place and was observed assiduously by all. It was an incredible

---

1   See Anote Tong, *Preliminary Statement by the Chair*, Commonwealth Observer Group Bougainville Referendum, Buka, 11 December 2019, production-new-commonwealth-files.s3.eu-west-2.amazon aws.com/migrated/inline/Commonwealth%20Observer%20Group%20to%20Bougainville%20-%20 PreliminaryStatement.pdf.

2   McKenna et al., 'Bougainville Referendum'.

indication of what could be regulated and enforced in Bougainville when there was community support. As Anthony Regan, Kerryn Baker and Thiago Opperman observe:

> The success of the referendum as an electoral process is in large part due to the strong community support for the referendum process … The impact of the remarkable engagement by Bougainvilleans in awareness and reconciliation and other referendum-related activities cannot be [overestimated].[3]

I met Eddie on the deck at Reasons, overlooking the water, where he was drinking a Coca-Cola. The pizza oven was still as it was in 2016 but was now covered in dust, and the beer fridges were as empty as an open tabernacle. Eddie looked contented. These weeks had been a destination for at least 30 years, and they were the result of the work undertaken by community leaders like himself in the previous years. I asked Eddie what he thought the result would be; he was bullish that it was going to be for independence. 'No-one is supporting "greater autonomy". That's just the same rubbish that we have now. It's independence, for sure.'

There were two choices on the ballot before Bougainvilleans: 'independence' and 'greater autonomy'. We had spent days in those various Post-Referendum Planning Task-Force meetings trying to elaborate the definitions[4] of these terms, but to no avail. It didn't seem to matter very much on the ground, however. I had lived through the vote to ratify the Good Friday peace agreement in Northern Ireland, Brexit in the wider United Kingdom, and gay marriage in Australia – all of which saw impassioned people making 'pro' and 'con' arguments – but for this referendum there was no campaign at all, no-one making an argument for sticking or twisting, no-one who seemed bothered about questions of financial viability.[5] There was much active campaigning on independence, and no-one seemed to be making the case for greater autonomy. As Regan, Baker and Opperman observe in their analysis of the referendum period, the absences of any 'anti-independence' voices would have been unthinkable even a few years earlier and represented

---

3   Anthony J. Regan, Kerryn Baker and Thiago Cintra Oppermann, 'The 2019 Bougainville Referendum and the Question of Independence: From Conflict to Consensus', *The Journal of Pacific History* 57, no. 1 (2022): 26, 30, doi.org/10.1080/00223344.2021.2010683.

4   'Descriptions of the Bougainville Referendum Options', Papua New Guinea and Autonomous Bougainville Government, www.abg.gov.pg/images/news/011119_Final_Detailed_descriptions_of_options.pdf.

5   Chand, *Fiscal Autonomy.*

a remarkable turnaround from the divisions over Bougainville's political future that helped partly fuel 'the Crisis' and which continued following the Peace Agreement.[6]

While the riches under the ground would be enough to bankroll a place of this size. The mine remained resolutely shut, serving in the referendum as little more than an arresting backdrop for news reports. No concerns were apparent as to who was going to do the work, or the lack of people with public administration skills to work through and set up new government arrangements. No-one in Buka was descending into a discussion of such encumbrances.

I called into one of the government offices to collect a commemorative T-shirt, which came in 3XL and gave me the look of one of those men in Weight Watchers advertisements wearing an old shirt to illustrate the number of pounds shed. Inside the office, the standard lethargy prevailed. Someone was typing out with one finger a letter to the minister on behalf of the cleaner requesting extra allowances; the man beside him was simply staring inertly into space. Everyone here, too, was confident of a vote for independence.

'What happens next?' I asked.

'We'll work on that next year,' the man staring into space answered, with certitude.

---

6   Regan, Baker and Opperman, 'The 2019 Bougainville Referendum'.

16

The stone pillars

By the end of the first of the two weeks of the referendum, most people had voted, and polling stations erected around town started to be dismantled. There was nothing much else for anyone to do but wait. I wrote a couple of articles for Australian blogging platforms and read a few crime novels borrowed from the library to pass the time before counting began.

However, I knew that this might be my last stint in Bougainville for a while, and I didn't want to leave without seeing the stones.

One of the most intriguing parts of *Both Sides of Buka Passage* is close to the end, when Beatrice admits that she can find no explanation for a series of pillars, stones and dolmens a few feet in height that stood erect in random places on Buka Island and in the northern part of Bougainville Island. Something about these stones put this scrupulously studious anthropologist off balance. In contrast to the unleavened style of the rest of her book, Beatrice wrote about the stones in a manner almost approaching the giddy. There was nothing natural about these pillars, she asserted; they showed 'definite signs of human handiwork', some smoothed down into the sheen of marble and others with designs reminiscent of honeycomb incised into them. At a small village she called Tohatchi (known later as Tohatsi), she found a stone that was about six feet high, with diamond-shaped marks near the base; she took pictures of some local people standing by it, and they looked diminutive by contrast. Close by, she discovered a set of stones known as '*A Pi*'.[1] 'Pi' means 'sores', and it was feared by locals that boils and suppurating wounds would break

---

1   Blackwood, *Both Sides of Buka Passage*, 533.

out on anyone who touched the *A Pi*. Beatrice was having none of what she plainly regarded as mumbo-jumbo, and she rubbed away mud, moss and lichens from one of the stones. She told her companions that she had 'destroyed its evil power by cleaning it', saying in her account:

> [T]hey were then emboldened to lift it out of the thicket of bush which grew round it and put it in a position where I could photograph it, and even to hold it upright while I did so … They said that now I had cleaned it they would not be afraid of it any more.[2]

The true meanings of these stones, and why they were positioned as they were, eluded Beatrice. Her normally voluble and loquacious informants seemed unusually reluctant to stump up explanations. 'Were they phallic, some sort of shrines, even places of human sacrifice?' she speculated, wildly. Why was everyone pretending they weren't important? Most remarkably, in a place where everything had a ritual significance of some sort, she found that many people claimed not to have even been aware of these unusual stones in their midst prior to her pointing them out. This also struck me as odd. In villages where everyone knew everyone's business and lineage, where every stone had meaning, how could stones with unusual markings not have some sort of story attached to them?

Eddie had heard of the stone pillar at Tohatsi and had visited there when he was at school. He had been told it was an arrow fired from a nearby island – but of the stones known as *A Pi*, he, too, said he knew nothing. I believed him. I picked him up beside the giant screen. He had new headwear: a sort of pork pie hat. We were joined by Sylvester, another ex-combatant.

We drove out past the airport and the new little strips of shops opposite; past the office of the president, the Bougainville parliament and the now forsaken government offices, one of which was the office where I had begun, the one that had once contained the voluminous files of my antecedents. The offices had been abandoned when the government refused to pay rent to one of their ministers, who had provided the building in his previous incarnation as the regional member in the National Parliament. The minister's men arrived, told everyone to get out, and stripped the innards of the building. The walls to my office were knocked through, the untold amounts of bureaucratic miseries in the compilations of all those papers and reports scattered to the ground, stamped on, and, over time, ground

---

2   Blackwood, *Both Sides of Buka Passage*, 533.

down into the dust. The minister in question remained in Cabinet for a while afterwards, 'working around the clock' to get the government to lease the building back.

We also drove past the red roof of the new location of the Unity library, painted in the bright colours of Digicel, the mobile phone company that had sponsored its new location. On this day, as on so many days I'd seen before, there was a little queue of children outside. Leslie the librarian and her husband, Pat, who managed the law and justice program, had just left; I'd been to their leaving do the day before. It was a joyous affair, but what would stay with me the most was a speech from one of Pat's early counterparts, now a retired magistrate. He said that in all his years, Pat was the first white man who hadn't shouted at him.

On we went, past a pizzeria managed by nuns. The dough is made to a Viennese recipe, the legacy of an Austrian aid worker who had been here for many years and whom I felt certain was likely to leave more of a lasting legacy than I would. Just past the pizzeria came a half-built building; meant to be Bougainville's first polytechnic, it was another incomplete project courtesy of the local MP who had sponsored the Filipino ghost ship.

An hour up the road was the village of Tohatsi, the place where Beatrice had found the stones. We had arranged to meet Joel, a secondary-school teacher and member of the clan on whose land the various stones rested, who was going to show us around. Joel was a former heavyweight boxer, and his torso was shredded like a tractor engine. Eddie had been in touch with him, and he was happy to help in return for a copy of Beatrice's book.

Finding the stone pillar at Tohatsi was a cinch. It was standing in clear sight by the side of the road, its hieroglyphs, grooves and markings more weather-beaten now than in Beatrice's time but still visible and distinct. The only difference was that the pillar was no longer upright but now at a precipitous 45-degree angle after a truck had smashed into it a few years before. The truck emerged second best from the encounter and was rendered immobile.

Just like the villagers back in Beatrice's time, Joel said he had not heard of the *A Pi* stones either. They weren't on the stretch of road where Beatrice had photographed and left them. The first five people we asked said they had never heard of them and gave us looks to indicate they thought we were all a little crazy. Some of those we asked were adamant: they had never heard of these stones and they were the ones more likely to know if any were around, rather than some fellow who had just arrived with an annotated copy of a big book. The local chief deadpanned that he knew of them but didn't know where they were. A man behind him listening in on our conversation scowled. I had a rising feeling that we were being given the run-around but couldn't quite work out why. The office-bearers of the village institution were holding out.

It was a teenage boy wearing a Korn T-shirt and carrying a bush knife who let us in on the secret. The stones did exist. There were originally four, but now there were only three, and he knew where to find them. He warned us they no longer looked like the pictures I showed him in Beatrice's book. We drove a few hundred yards back down the road, walked into the jungle and a few minutes later came across a pit in the ground covered with bamboo reeds, coconut husks, branches, the petals from what looked like chrysanthemums, and shavings of bark. The boy pointed down and, through Eddie, explained that the stones were now buried far underneath.

Before the white man's war, he said, the stones had been exposed for a few years 'after some white' had dug them up, with calamitous consequences. Throughout all the time they were visible, the people in the village had broken out in sores, boils and unexplained wounds that neither bush medicine nor drugs from the doctor could heal. Was this 'white' Blackwood, I wondered? Either no-one seemed to know, or no-one wanted to tell me, ruining the chance of a definitive denouement to the mystery. He went on to explain that once they had tried everything else, the villagers decided to bury the stone pillars deep in the earth and never to unearth them again for anyone who came asking about them. Were people still breaking out in sores? A few were, but not as many as when the stone slabs sat astride the earth. Would the pillars ever be dug up again? No, they would not. The photographs of the ornate swirls and pattern of lines of the *A Pi* in Beatrice's book will remain the only visuals of these intriguing stones. The chief looked at me with some concern – I assured him I wasn't planning to dig them up. I asked him if he'd voted yet, and he said he and the whole village had voted on the first day. I asked for his prediction of the result. 'Independence,' he said. 'We'll have it by Christmas'.

On the way back down to Buka, we stopped for Eddie to buy betel nut, and he pointed to two men out for a walk. 'I bet you don't know what they are doing,' he said, thumbing in their direction. 'They are making a curse,' I replied, confidently. 'How do you know that, white man?' he asked, surprised. 'Beatrice wrote about it,' I said.

17

The result of all this

The counting and announcement of the result took place at the high-school hall on the outskirts of Buka where I had first met Dennis.

I had been tweeting pictures from Bougainville during the referendum weeks: the flag flying from various incongruous locations; a positive review of the bakery's meat pies; a picture of the dusty pizza oven that had stayed under the steps of Reasons for the last four years because it was too heavy to carry up the creaky stairs; a picture of Eddie and some other ex-combatants looking gruffly into the camera, along with his potted biography. This diverse photo-play brought me into the orbit of Bloomberg, *The Times* of London and various Australian media outlets, each hoping for someone to give them on-the-ground reactions to the result. Endeavouring to be of service, I went down to the count with a fully charged phone and, crucially, the passcode to get me access to the Referendum Commission's satellite wi-fi connection.

One of the first people I ran into was the Honourable Joseph Watawi, wearing a new camouflage green hat bearing the words, 'Fish tremble when they hear me roar'. Various diplomat types dressed in official-looking safari jackets milled around. Eddie strode in a few minutes later, and shortly afterwards, a caravanserai of worthies arrived: Bougainville's president, various ministers, sundry members of Bougainville's House of Representatives, and the Papua New Guinean minister for Bougainville affairs. Also present were six of the seven referendum commissioners who had organised the referendum, all bedecked with official shirts. Bertie Ahern, former Irish prime minister who headed the independent commission that managed the referendum, was slathered in so much sunscreen he looked like the corpse at a wake. After a bit of milling around, we were ready to start. By now, the humidity levels in the hall were close to 100 per cent.

We started half an hour later. First there was a prayer, then there was a preacher, then there were anthems, then there was a statement thanking every conceivable person, and then the former Irish prime minister stood up to announce the result.

It was a landslide. Of the more than 180,000 votes cast, 178,000 had opted for independence. It was, with only one exception (South Sudan), the largest 'pro' vote for independence in any such vote anywhere in the world. Some cheers echoed within the hall, not cacophonous by any means and then, soon afterwards, about 20 women in the middle of the hall broke out in a hymn.

I'd been expecting euphoria, but the initial reaction seemed oddly muted.

My phone lit up with requests for on-the-ground favours. I felt as excited as Beatrice would have been when she received the occasional letter exclaiming delight in her work. 'Can you find some people to talk to?' was always the request, so I lined up Joseph and Eddie, filming them on my iPhone as they talked like seasoned media professionals. They were relishing their place in the sun. 'All along the desire for independence was in my blood,' Eddie said to a CNN reporter in Hong Kong. 'It was what our ancestors always wanted … they wanted to make sure the issue of fighting for independence was put to rest.' He was utterly sincere.

I drove into Buka expecting car-honking scenes of celebration and flags flying even higher than before, but there was nothing; the town was settling back into its quiet slumber. It reminded me of driving on a Christmas afternoon: so much effort put into preparation followed by deflation. There was nothing to indicate that a referendum had even happened. The beer shops were still shut, and even the mashed-up religious banner was gone. I went home, fixed myself a soda water and squeezed in a lime.

* * *

I left for Port Moresby a few days later, departing from Buka on the lunchtime flight. That morning I'd gone into the office to see Dennis, who was typing his resignation letter. I'd brought another bottle of whiskey up, intending to give it to Eddie, but thought, on balance, Dennis deserved it more. 'I'm leaving,' he said, meaning stepping aside, and I told him I was, too. He showed me the detailed resignation letter he'd written the night before, soul-penetrating in its sharp, sorrowful intensity. We shook hands. We should have hugged. He is the best of good men. Unlike Beatrice and me, he had no boat to get on, no plane to catch, no book to write. My contract would run out in April, and I didn't plan on renewing it. I had planned to write a travel book about PNG and Solomon Islands and had Eddie lined up to accompany me. Little did I know then how 2020 would unfold.

The terminal was sweaty bedlam. Referendum staff were heading home; the check-in machine was buggered up, so the staff were writing out tickets and luggage stubs by hand. I was glad to get my bum on a seat in the cabin. The route we would be taking was rare. Instead of banking immediately out onto the Solomon Sea for Port Moresby, we were bound for the airport in Arawa to pick up additional passengers. We sailed over the Buka Passage, and I looked down onto the dusty road cut out of the lush green. We would have passed Kurtatchi soon after but were too high up to see it. On our right was the Crown Prince Range that the German administrators named from afar, and within there, somewhere, shrouded by clouds, was Panguna.

Arawa's airport had been built to service the mining operations. Closed for many years, it reopened in 2014. A small jet was parked on the airport's apron, the plane of the prime minister of PNG, who was (I was following the events on social media) addressing a rapturous crowd at the park in Arawa. His name was James Marape. Marape had been finance minister but had resigned, assembling a coalition to topple the incumbent and taken over himself. He was a Sabbath-observing Seventh Day Adventist whose aspiration was to make his country the world's 'richest Black Christian nation'. His works were twists on donor speak. Upon taking office, he'd published his 'Marape Manifesto', an eight-page collection of high-sounding phrases and catchwords spliced from the books of the Bible and tomes of aid bureaucrats. The document outlined 10 broad goals ranging from 'We will endeavour to build our military, our police, our correction services into self-sufficient and disciplined revenue earners for our country so that they keep our external borders and domestic economy secure' to 'The God of Abraham, Isaac and Jacob will be the God of Papua New Guinea'. It rounds off with a concluding statement to chill the hearts of report-writers all over Moresby: 'These mantra, aims and manifestos are from the core of my DNA and not from data, statistics or policy evidence.'

A large part of me saluted the prime minister for having the courage to put his unvarnished thoughts down on paper. Few political leaders in any countries do that, and there was none of the fakery here that appears in other official government documents, few of which give the impression of having been read by the people named as having written them. His manifesto showed Messianic faith in the power of the state, despite all evidence to the contrary. There were no nuts-and-bolts details in his manifesto, no tarrying on details such as who was going to do the work or how it was going to be done, nothing about boring subjects like planning or logistics. It was just all going to happen, somehow, like a miracle. One of his advisers told me that Marape sincerely believed that he had been put on this earth to fulfil God's plan.

On this particular day, the man whose country Bougainvilleans so emphatically voted to leave received a hero's welcome and arrived brandishing a dummy cheque for 50 million kina (A$20 million). He spoke in beguiling aphorisms about 'economic independence', finding a 'sweet spot between independence and autonomy' and about how he, as a simple man, didn't have an opinion on Bougainville's future. Eddie was down there in some unspecified security provision fashion, and I hoped that for once, he'd be paid for his services. A years-long research project lay in trying to disentangle the contradictions of it all.

As we flew on for Moresby, I thought about Beatrice, the ghosts of Australiana in Arawa, and Bougainville's uncertain future. By few objective criteria could it be said that Bougainville was ready to be independent if one took as one's start and end point the government in Buka. But looking at the men and the villagers who had buried the *A Pi* stones, their compatriots with shovels and trowels up in Panguna, or the fishermen and women at Pororan, I wondered if such air-conditioned judgements really mattered. Government was entirely absent from all their lives. They expected little or nothing of it, be it an administration in Buka or Port Moresby, and they received little or nothing in return. These were the true institutions.

Bougainvilleans are people who are, to all intents and purposes, already autonomous and independent. Will it really make a material difference to the people's lives which government sits far away? Holy Moses: it will not.

Epilogue

I returned to Port Moresby a few months later for what I didn't know then was the last week BC (Before COVID). I had a few days' work to finish, and when that was done I spent a few days going through the archives at Papua New Guinea's National Library. The library was one of the independence gifts from Australia in 1975, the era reflected in its decor and brutalist architectural style. The noticeboards were made of red felt, the signage was old-fashioned, and the building's interior corners were shrouded in demi-darkness. This was a functioning and well-frequented library, albeit a poorly resourced one. Not many books seemed to have been purchased in the last 20 years. Most patrons were writing notes in jotters; a couple of people were working on laptops. Only one person was playing with their phone. I spent happy days reading old copies of the *Arawa Bulletin* and some old government documents.

Naturally, I was staying at the Holiday Inn, and, naturally, there was another hefty delegation from Bougainville staying there also. They were in town for a meeting of the JSB, and the primary agenda item they were pushing seemed abstruse in nature: to change the name of the JSB to 'Joint Consultative Body'. There seemed to be no urgency to progress the actual results of the referendum. By contrast, three months after a similar referendum in the then Indonesian-occupied province of East Timor, the Indonesians had left, and a United Nations administration was in charge of administering the territory.[1] (This is far from a perfect comparison; the Indonesians laid waste to Dili and other parts of the country before they left. No violence occurred after Bougainville's referendum.)

---

[1]   The approach of 'consultative referendum' followed by a parliamentary decision was modelled on East Timor, an approach credited to the Australian foreign minister of the time, Alexander Downer. See Anthony Regan, 'The Bougainville Referendum Arrangements: Origins, Shaping and Implementation: Part One: Origins and Shaping' (Australian Aid, Pacific Research Program, Discussion Paper 2018/4), openresearch-repository.anu.edu.au/bitstream/1885/147139/1/DPA%20DP2018_4%20Regan%20 pt%201%20final.pdf.

As per the Peace Agreement, the two parties were meant to 'consult' on the referendum result, with the outcome of that consultation going to the parliament of PNG for final decision-making. No such consultation had begun. I ran into Joseph Watawi at the little shop inside the Inn, where he was buying phone credit and getting his change in packets of chewing gum. He had backflipped since we'd last seen each other; he'd joined the government and was now its minister for economic development. Joseph rattled off the policies he was going to enact: tax reform, support for small and medium enterprises, improved access to credit. 'I have told my technical officers to stop sleeping and get to work,' he said. I did not know then, but it was the last time I would see him.

As it turned out, there would be no 'work' for Joseph's staff to get back to. In response to curtailing the spread of COVID-19, the government shut down about a week later. All but a few of the expatriates and national advisers had been evacuated and the daily flight from Moresby cancelled. The island was effectively independent, cut off (apart from mobile phone signals) from the outside world. The government in Port Moresby gave the government in Buka some money to support its efforts to thwart COVID, which parliamentarians allocated to their own campaigning, with no hint of irony for 'awareness', when, presumably, a large gathering could itself be a potential superspreader event.

The election for the new Bougainville legislature and president began in late August 2020, with counting beginning in the middle of September. Results were being sent to my phone by the minute. The elections were well-organised; the count staff worked well past 4:06 without complaint. The reason for this dedication was not that Bougainvilleans were somehow better at organising elections than other things: it was the fact that everyone had an interest in the outcome. I wondered how could such enthusiasm, commitment and skill be bottled for the everyday work of government.

Many of my friends were vying for seats. Eddie ran in his constituency and fell short, as did Dennis in his, coming a close second. Joseph was defeated by a medical doctor.

There was a wide field of runners and riders aiming to be president, including ex-combatants, some of the bureaucrats who had been turfed out of office for financial chicanery, a former minister and owner of the Oasis nightclub, the former speaker of the parliament, a sports administrator, a rocket scientist, and even the man from the psychedelic presentation about the Strategic Development Plan. (He had been appointed acting chief secretary after Nobetau's dismissal.) All ran on effectively the same platform: that they were the one person who was best positioned to deliver on the referendum result. No-one mentioned the Strategic Development Plan.

Emerging victorious was Ishmael Toroama, a former leader of the BRA, signatory to the Peace Agreement and prominent in 'a wide variety of fields of endeavour', including 'weapons disposal, business, music, church'.[2]

There is no doubting the sincerity of this man in his desire to lead his people to independence. Negotiations with PNG are proceeding, slowly, with a commitment to determining a political settlement between 2025 and 2027.

Profound structural issues with the public service remain, leaving wide open the question as to who is going to do the practical work to fill in the detail of this new settlement: developing the position papers, working on the exposure drafts, and overseeing the grinding, frequently dull, fiendishly complex and eminently necessary minutiae of bureaucracy, policy and law. The question of 'who' is often overlooked. Few bureaucrats anywhere in the world could straightforwardly take on the challenge of negotiating new governmental arrangements for a new state, and that includes the public servants of Buka and Port Moresby. In 2022, Joseph Mona, Bougainville's minister for public service, lamented ingrained work practices. The *Post Courier* quoted him thus: 'In the ABG public service, we start work late and knock off early, putting in only 25 hours a week at most.' Mona questioned 'how the nation will be able to achieve its dreams of becoming an independent nation when we are at our lowest levels in terms of our performance'.[3] Former chief secretary Nobetau wrote in 2022: 'The challenge is to now migrate from a mindset of aspiration to one of implementation.'[4]

2   Anthony Regan, 'An Assessment of Bougainville's President Toroama Part Two: Business and Music Activities', *Department of Pacific Affairs In Brief* 13 (2021), bellschool.anu.edu.au/sites/default/files/publications/attachments/2021-05/an_assessment_of_bougainvilles_president_toroama_part_two_-_business_and_music_activites_in_brief_2021_13_anthony_regan_department_of_pacific_affairs.pdf.
3   Romulus Masiu, 'Mona Urges Public Servants to be Effective', *Post Courier*, 10 February 2022.
4   Joseph Nobetau, 'Bougainville Parliament Prevents Public Service Politicisation', *Devpolicy* (blog), 1 March 2022, devpolicy.org/bougainville-parliament-prevents-public-service-politicisation-20220301/.

It seems obvious that some external support will be required, but the question is whether, in terms of *realpolitik*, other states will want to lend a hand.

Tied to this question is the issue of what the terms of any settlement should look like, and how it would be prepared. It was a scenario I'd try to run bureaucrats through a number of times when I worked there:

> OK, you're now negotiating after the result. You get flown to Port Moresby, put up in the Holiday Inn and have to start negotiating the next day. What do you ask for first? In the case of Brexit, the UK negotiators focused on fisheries, trade deals and borders during their talks with the Europeans. What about Bougainville?

It was always hard to get a concrete answer; I'd hear phrases like 'transitional arrangements' and 'sign a treaty', but it was difficult to get into specifics. I've often wondered why it was so hard to descend into details. Was it that Bougainville had never had to think about anything like this in the past? Was it their lack of exposure to other functioning government models? Was this not the way they would go about decision-making in their own society? Finding answers to these questions will be important if the Bougainvilleans are to forge the type of detailed separation agreement that they aspire to in their negotiations.

There are many potential starting points for consultations. Here are a few:

- agreeing on the additional governmental powers and functions that will or could be transferred to Bougainville, along with a timeline for transfer and a budget for their cost
- determining what support the Bougainville government will need to enable it to exercise its responsibilities effectively
- working out financial arrangements between Bougainville and PNG
- animating hitherto dormant provisions of the Peace Agreement pertaining to revenue-sharing for fisheries.

It needs to be clear that there is no right or wrong place to start – and that it is all going to be technical in nature. What matters most is to start somewhere.

In the first year of its tenure, the Toroama government's main problem was something that it could not negotiate or sign an MoU with: a roiling COVID-19 virus that ripped through this would-be nation. The whole of PNG managed to dodge the worst of COVID in 2020, only to be clobbered with a vengeance in 2021. It pains me that many of the people I worked with during my time here and have referenced in this book are now to be referred to in the past tense. John Tabinaman, the lands minister, passed away, as did other senior Bougainvillean leaders, including former vice-president Raymond Masono, whose Master's thesis I had found in my office some years earlier. Joseph Watawi died in Buka hospital in November 2021. We had been messaging each other regularly; I'd tell him about my move to the United States, and he'd reply that he intended to come to Washington to make the case for Bougainville independence. Sadly, he never will.

Donor support continues, but with a different twist on the recipe used in the past. The present Australian iteration comes with a significant reduction in advisory support, with attention tilted more to the support of organisations in Bougainville that provide practical assistance. The position I held was discontinued. More broadly, the debate on the value of technical assistance continues. It remains an impossible task to define. It would be more realistic to adopt the *brukim bus* strategy, accepting that this will be long-term drudgery, in which there will be much sitting around, much everyday frustration, and occasional frenetic bouts of activity and accomplishment. We need to find a better vocabulary to define and explain this sort of long-haul, much-needed, foundational but unheralded work.

For now, this would-be nation, this unsung land, remains in limbo between where it is and where its voters want it to be. Is this place ready for independence? I'll answer the question by asking another: was any country ready for independence when it gained it? Some countries in the Pacific (and, indeed, elsewhere in the world) became independent not because they passed some form of competence test or aptitude test, but because the colonial powers that once ruled them decided, on their terms, that it was time for them to go. Bougainville has a harder challenge than states that became independent in the colonial sunset. It will have to prove it is ready more than others did, notwithstanding that most individual Bougainvilleans are independent people already, both in their willingness to be responsible for their lives and in their spirit.

Glossary

A Pi   name given to a set of mysterious stones in Bougainville, first written about by English anthropologist Beatrice Blackwood

betel nut   seed of the Areca palm, chewed as a stimulant throughout Papua New Guinea, where it is known as *buai*

bikman (big man)   term used in Papua New Guinea to describe a leader (generally, although not always, a man) whose influence is associated with the ability to acquire and distribute resources to those he leads

blackskins   term used by people from other parts of Papua New Guinea to describe Bougainvilleans

bonito   fish belonging to the tuna family

brukim bus   'to cut one's way through thick bush', a metaphor for the business of government or administration

Buka Town   urban and administrative hub of the Autonomous Region of Bougainville, located on Buka Island (Buka), just off the main island of Bougainville

cicastration   an ornate process of body tattooing by which marks were made on the skin with flints of glass and coral

cocovore   person who eats only coconuts

the Crisis   violent conflict in Bougainville, 1988–97. Part ethno-nationalist in nature, it pitted Bougainvilleans against the Papua New Guinea army and police, while other elements were more akin to an intra-Bougainvillean civil conflict. A 2001 Peace Agreement formally ended the Crisis

go pinis	leaving, to leave
IKEA	global furniture retail company selling affordable home and office furniture
Japanese Zero	plane used by the Japanese in the Second World War
kai bar	place where one can buy prepared food (Papua New Guinea)
luluai	village chief, tribal chief (appointed by a colonial administration)
MSG	monosodium glutamate, a flavour enhancer added to some restaurant foods
pasim maus	'shut mouth' (keeping quiet, not divulging information)
redskins	term used by Bougainvilleans to describe people from other parts of Papua New Guinea
sigil	pictorial symbol believed to hold magical power
singsing	group singing, often associated with ceremonial dancing and feasting
Tok Pisin	Papua New Guinean Pidgin, the lingua franca of Papua New Guinea
upe	headdress worn by teenage boys in certain parts of Bougainville during a period of initiation
urar	spirits of the dead
Wedgewood	traditional English producer of fine china and earthenware popular in Australia in the 20th century

www.ingramcontent.com/pod-product-compliance
Lightning Source LLC
Chambersburg PA
CBHW050844270326

41930CB00020B/3460